SUFFERING IN
SILENCE

RECOGNIZING THAT YOU ARE NOT ALONE

Cornelius Lindsey

DEDICATION

I would like to dedicate this book to each congregant at The Gathering Oasis Church. I am honored to serve as your pastor. It is my prayer and earnest expectation that each congregant remains present and active. I pray you grow more and more in the power of the Lord. It is my assignment to prepare each of you for eternity. At the end of my life, I pray I have done what God has purposed for me to do.

TABLE OF CONTENTS

Snype~ Alan
Chester

I Sell Books
✓ CE for Pastor
Lifetime Membership

INTRODUCTION

Here is my heartfelt cry and desperate attempt to get you to finally confront the truth that stares you in the face every day. My objective is to challenge you in such a way with truth that you are left with no other choice but to examine your current way of living and make the appropriate changes. This book is purposed for your freedom. Understand that I cannot give you freedom-- only Jesus can. He draws and compels you with love. He does not just fill you; He encounters you. He changes you from the inside out. You must yield yourself to Him. I know enduring pain is difficult. I want you to know that you do not have to live with the pain and silent sufferings any longer. You do not have to live in fear. You do not have to suffer in silence. Please know that you are not alone.

On April 24, 2014, a young man walked into a classroom filled with students. The instructor was waiting to begin her lecture for the day. "Take your seat! " she exclaimed. He was a slender fellow with a beautiful head of hair, brilliant light blue eyes, a playful smile, and pearly white teeth. The women would swoon over him every place he traveled. As he sat down he noticed a young woman sitting next to him. He politely asked her if he could borrow a pen for class. "No!" she quietly snapped back at him. He turned to the other side to a young man of Middle Eastern descent. He quietly asked if he could borrow a pen from him. "Sure, you can have it. I have more."

As the young man sat there in class he could not help but think about the snappy response from the young lady next to him and the rather polite gesture from the guy on his other side. As class came to an end he turned to the young lady and asked her if everyone was okay. "Yes, I'm great. Everything is fine," she said to him. "Are you sure?" said the young man. "Look, I said I'm fine!" shouted the young woman as she grabbed her things and stormed out the classroom. He did not know if something was wrong with her but he did know something was not right.

He noticed her designer bag, latest model laptop, most up-to-date phone, and all the accessories many people would love to have but could not afford. She was remarkably beautiful. He could not understand why she was so upset. He had noticed her in past classes sporting a gorgeous smile and walking with some of the most beautiful women he had every seen. She drove the newest Mercedes Benz around campus. It was white with a peanut butter interior. She was very noticeable, and everyone noticed her and everything she had. She looked like she had it all, but what was the problem? What he did not know was that she was very insecure.

The makeup, designer clothes and bags, latest accessories, and everything else helped to cover the torment warring in her heart. What he did not know was the story about how she was raped by a crowd of young men at a late night party. She had gone as a favor to her friend who did not want to go alone. One of the guys spiked her drink, which made her unable to think soberly. As she was passing out the young men took turns raping her. She woke up the next morning in tears. The shame and embarrassment of the entire situation was too much for her to handle. She wished she had died instead of woken up from that awful nightmare. The anger in her heart towards the young men stemmed from a deeply rooted bitterness towards men. He also did not know she was upset because she felt alone.

Although she was around people, she felt like people did not really know her or her private struggles. Some would say she just did not want to be bothered.

The pain from her past was deep, and it was compounded by other issues that stemmed from events that occurred earlier in the day. The moment her tire went flat and her alarm did not go off--which made her late for work--triggered that anger that sat dormant in her heart. Asking for the pen was the tip of the iceberg. To him, it was just a pen. To her, it was asking for her whole life--like he was trying to take something from her that did not belong to him just like those boys had done to her years ago.

There was a young African-American man who sat towards the back of the class that day. He was so uninterested in anything that was being taught. There would be times when he would just fall asleep. Like the young lady, he had the best clothes, the nicest car in the parking lot, and everything anyone could ask for. People knew his parents were financially wealthy. His dad served as the CEO of a major hedge fund for more than seventeen years. His father was worth a whopping 47 million dollars. His mother was a stay-at-home mom who did all she could to cater to her son's needs. The dad constantly encouraged him to finish college, achieve athletically, and be great at whatever he wanted his son to do.

The young man, named Antonio, had everything his heart could desire. He has traveled all over the world. His parent's home looked like something from a movie. He had his own boat docked outside one of his dad's lake houses. Antonio had it all. He also had a serious drug addiction. After being sent off to boarding school, he developed a drug habit that continued to advance throughout the years. He has been to some of the most renowned therapists in the country. His parents tried to give him everything he wanted so he would not have to turn to drugs. His dad, the more forceful of Antonio's parents, would get so angry at him because of his poor decisions.

One night, after Antonio was arrested for grand theft auto his dad bailed him out. "How could you? Are you crazy or something! Your mom and I have given you the world. We have sent you to the best schools. You have the nicest car. You have everything you could ever imagine; yet, you do this! What is wrong with you?" shouted Antonio's father. Wiping tears from his face, Antonio inhaled deeply and said, "I never asked you for any of that stuff. I did not want to go to boarding school. I never asked to play golf or lacrosse. I do not like those sports anyway. You want to know what I have wanted all my life? Huh? Do you? Do you, dad? I wanted YOU! I wanted you, dad! I wanted you to teach me how to play basketball. I wanted you to take me to the park down the street, not to the places around the world. I wanted you at my games, not taking me to professional games to sit around your hedge fund buddies! I wanted you to sit and talk to me, not expect my teachers to talk to me. I wanted you, not your money. The boy you see now is a product of your absence. I want to be relevant to you. I hate feeling like I am just another investment in your portfolio!"

Antonio started to cry, so he put his hands on his face to capture the tears that were running down his cheeks. Like a lot of children, Antonio did not want the things; he wanted his parents. There he was sitting in the class gazing deeply at the board as the instructor taught. His body was there, but his mind was far away. You could see the hurt and pain on his face. His struggles, although noticeable to those who really looked at him, were private. He was struggling in silence.

The eyes have the potential of containing an entire universe of silent exploration, if you take the time to look. I've often wondered what lies behind the eyes of men and women. I have walked the streets of Manhattan, London, Phoenix, Miami, Atlanta, San Juan, Nassau, and so many other places noticing the blank stares of women and men as they walked along the city streets. Many of them walked with such determination. I could only imagine if their destination was worth all the trouble it took to get there.

I oftentimes wonder about the daily struggles of men and women. I wonder about their past and the difficulties they have had to overcome. I wonder about their present life circumstances and the situations they have had to encounter to get them to that place. I wonder about their life and dreams and goals. I also wonder about their knowledge of the Lord Jesus Christ. I wonder if they go home to suffer in silence.

I think about the husband and father who dreads going

home because of is nagging wife and rebellious, hen-pecked children but does it out of obligation instead of desire. I wonder about the wife who is afraid to speak her opinions in fear that she will be slapped across the face again. I wonder about the niece who has been forced to endure the sexual abuse inflicted upon her by her uncle. Her suffering is silent like all the others.

I wonder about the young man who is afraid to speak out about being molested when he was younger. Instead, he hides himself in his room choosing to be distant from the world.

I wonder about the middle-aged man who chooses to party and chase loose women like his father did for so many years. He grew up saying he would never be like his father. Maybe that is why he is afraid to look in the mirror.

I wonder what little girl will hide in her closet tonight to hide from her stepfather or the little boy who has to watch as his dad hits his mom again and again and again.

I wonder how many will suffer in silence because they feel so alone. Do they feel abandoned by the world?

Finally, I wonder if you--yes, you—the one reading this book think you are all alone. Do you? Do you see a part of yourself in something you have already read? Have these words already pricked something in your heart? Have you grown so numb to the pain that you have accepted it as normal and something to you just have to live in? Some have gone from being abused to abusing others. Now, all of your relationships look like what you once hated. Well, I want you to know you are not alone.

I do not have all the answers. In fact, I am working out my own salvation like you. What I do have are personal experiences

I am willing to share with you in the hope that you will know YOU ARE NOT ALONE. Let's take off our personal masks, get down to the naked truth and confront the areas of our lives we have tried to hide for so long. Let's start the conversation about the lack of transparency in the Church and the world-at-large. It is time for you to break the bondage to those around you and the opinions they hold of you, be open with your addictions and your desire to end them, and so much more. It is time. God is with you all the way. Be encouraged.

Chapter 1

SUFFERING IN SILENCE

I oftentimes sit and think about the innocent who are left without a voice. Their screams go unheard; their call for help, unanswered. I cannot help but think about the young girl who sits in a corner every night crying her eyes out because she does not want to endure another round of sexual exploitation from her stepfather. I think about the young man who wears of mask of piety and becomes a master at religion to cover up the lust in his heart.

I think about the father who searches all day for a place to work so he can make a decent living. He wants to be able to provide for his family. He rises early in the morning and does not retire to bed until late at night. He is not lazy. He is not full of excuses. He does all he can and all he knows to provide for his loved ones, but he still goes home empty-handed. His wife and children have learned what it means to be hungry and destitute. They know what it feels like to go to bed without food or water.

My heart breaks for the young man who searches the world for love and affection. His search leads him straight into the arms of a welcoming gang who is hell bent on institutionalizing him and turning him into a monster of epic proportions. They will provide a place where his anger can be cultivated and transformed into rage and murder. He goes from being the innocent child to a cold-bloodied killer.

I think about the young women who are traded in terrorist camps and used for sexual pleasure. I am constantly thinking about their pain and displeasure. They scream for help, but no one hears them. They cry out for comfort, but no one answers.

Because of this burden in my heart, there are times when I cannot find sleep. I stay awake all night tossing and turning until I have no other choice but to fall on my knees and pray. It is in that place of prayer that I am able to pour out my heart and seek peace and comfort from God. I do not have the means to provide for everyone, but I do have the ability to offer my greatest gift—time in prayer. Prayer is a private matter that has public reward. I truly believe God hears me and He answers according to His perfect will.

There are many who are suffering in silence, both in and out of the church. I do not mean the church building when I write "the church." I am speaking of the whole body of believers. I am sure those suffering depression within the church is very high, but it does not compare to the depression found outside of it. Believers have hope in Jesus Christ. We are able to look beyond this world and its problems. That is not true for unbelievers. Their hope is temporal; it has an expiration date. My heart breaks for them and yearns for the illumination of their heart and mind.

I believe depression is a very real emotional disorder that has the power to affect a person's thoughts, behavior and entire sense of well-being. It is so strong that it can pull a person in a downward direction. I have felt it many times in my life. It is like a weight that sits atop your shoulders. It gets heavier and heavier as it continues to live inside of you. It drives you to become anti-social and less communicative. The longer it lasts the more you difficult it is to get out of bed and perform the regular activities you are accustomed to doing.

While out sharing the Gospel, I met an older woman in her late sixties who suffered greatly from depression. She was very active in her local church, giving the majority of her time to volunteer work. She woke up every morning to get dressed and made sure her grandchildren were off to school. Presently, she has been left to raise them on her own since her only daughter is lost to the streets due to a terrible drug habit. She worries a great deal because she does not know how she is going to feed her grandchildren, or herself, most days. It is difficult for her to talk about her struggles.

She is well educated with very high credentials. She oftentimes thinks she is over qualified for most positions and oftentimes dismissed because of her age. Her expenses include her mortgage, utilities, student loans, and a credit card she uses in emergency situations. Those expenses are well over $3,000 a month, but it does not include her food. She is barely able to pay all of her expenses on her part-time salary and few hours she works as a consultant for a small book-publishing firm. She also receives a decent $1,300 a month from Social Security because she is has been a widow of almost sixteen years. It does not help that she was recently mugged when a young man in his teens grabbed her pocketbook and threw her to the ground. She fractured her shoulder and tore her biceps. Her part-time job covers her physical therapy, but it will run out soon. Her injuries make it difficult to do many of the things she used to do. She now depends on her grandchildren for support. Unfortunately her grandson is focused on women and fast money. Her granddaughter does everything she can to assist her grandmother, but she fights a very real internal battle of trying to be popular and well-liked by the boys at her school.

Both of the grandkids deal with the anger of being abandoned by their mother and not knowing their father. The grandmother herds them to church every Sunday morning hoping the preacher will say something to impact their lives and change them for the better. The grandmother does not want to retire. She has too much life in her she has yet to live. She wants to work. She applies for work. She wants to be active. But no one is willing to hire her. Instead of sitting home and crying all day she volunteers her time at her local church. She feels broken and beaten at life. She hopes and prays her economic struggles are temporary. Her depression, although unwanted, is very real. Her tears are real. Her pain is real. And, in all of this she hides the diagnosis she received from her doctor. He gave her a short time to live. Even though her difficulties are great, she refuses to quit. Her hope is in the Lord; however, she fights a very real fight of depression.

As a pastor, I hear stories like this all the time. They are truly heartbreaking. I do everything in my power to help, but it sometimes seems my help is so minimal that it does little-to-nothing to help. I can easily give a hungry man a fish, but it will only feed him for a day. Teaching him how to fish—a task that takes patience and skill—enables him to fish for a lifetime. So what is the remedy? What is the method of fishing that must be taught in order for people like the grandmother to find comfort and peace in her situation? I believe it is being content, fully trusting God, and learning to serve others. I write a great deal in this book about being content, so I will not reveal it all here. I also write about trusting God. I want to use this part of the chapter to focus on serving others.

You may be reading this book and thinking that I have completely lost my mind. You maybe asking yourself how serving others is going to help someone who is depressed because of their personal situation. I believe the very root of depression—in this sense—can be selfishness. I understand there can be a medical component to depression, but I believe the remedy is still an honorable view of Christ, a selfless view towards others and a humble view of self. Depression is a constant thinking of self and focusing on what we cannot fix in our own ability. When all I have to focus on is why I am not able to do something then I lose sight of the struggles of others and my ability to use what I have to help them, even though I believe what I have is not enough. I honestly believe there is someone in the world that is going through something much worse than you or me. My worst day would be a great day for someone.

Serving others actually brings encouragement to self. It shows how much we actually have and how much we should be grateful for. You could be asking, "How could you be thankful seeing that you do not have any food?" You could still be thankful for a functioning mind and body. Instead of sitting idly by and being depressed you could go serve the homeless. It could very well happen that they provide you with a meal because of your service. In fact, you could forget about your hunger in the process because you are focused on serving someone else.

I have been in situations where I had to make a decision between paying my light bill and buying food. I was single at the time; however, I had a group of young men I mentored who were coming over to my house. These young guys were from different backgrounds, and some of them did not have the necessary means at their homes to eat. They were coming to my house for provision—even though I really did not have it. I chose to go buy groceries to feed the guys. I got in the kitchen and cooked that evening, served them the food, and cleaned up afterwards. I did not let anyone else know about my decision. I did not want to burden the young guys with my difficulties. I found so much joy in serving them and making sure they were fed and taken care of. I was willing to suffer in a house with no lights just so I could see them filled.

I went to the mailbox three days later after receiving a call from the electric company. They were telling me they were going to shut off my power. There was a check in the mail I was not expecting. It was for the exact amount of my electric power bill. My insurance company told me I had paid too much for my car insurance. They returned the overage to me. I was able to pay the electric bill and avoid my power being turned off. I could have very easily denied those young guys an opportunity to be fed, but I know my focus as a believer is to place the needs of others before myself.

Honestly, many of us have a very difficult time serving and helping others because we spend so much time looking at our lack. We focus on what we cannot do instead of looking at what we can do. Many also fall into a trap of depression because they do not properly direct their seed. They fail to understand that seed is not meant to be eaten; it is meant to be sown.

I want to give you an example to help you gain clarity of what I am saying. I was out preaching one evening at a small church in Minnesota. There had to be about fifteen people who attended that evening to hear the sermon. It was truly one of the greatest evenings of my life. Afterwards one of the men in the audience came up to me with tears in his eyes. He said, "Sir, I don't know who you are, but that sermon blessed me! I have to give you this!" He lifted my hand and placed a wad of 20s in it. I prayed with him and walked away towards my rental car.

On my way out of the church, I was walking towards the car and saw a husband and wife walking down the church steps. Nothing seemed to be wrong with them. The Holy Spirit immediately told me to give them the money that was just given to me. I had been in that situation time and time again, so it was not difficult to obey. I could have surely used the money though. I walked over to the couple and shook the husband's hand. We talked for a minute or two about the sermon. Then I lifted the husband's hand, took the wad of 20s out of my pocket, and put it in his. The man looked up at me and said, "Why are you doing this?" I told him I was led by the Holy Spirit to do it. His wife rushed over to me and gave me big hug. I shook the husband's hand, prayed with the both of them, and walked away towards my car.

As I get to my car, I hear the pastor of the church calling my name. "CORNELIUS! CORNELIUS!" he shouted. "Hold on a second!" He rushed over to me and asked me if I knew what was going on with that couple. I told him I did not. He proceeded to tell me the couple's situation. They had recently lost their jobs. They came to church earlier that day to serve. They did not ask for anything in return. However, the pastor knew they did not have any money. They were there to receive from God and trust Him at His word. Tears began to roll down my face because I just realized I was used by God as His servant to give as He directed. The money was not mine to keep. I have to constantly remember that God gives seed to the sower—even though we do not always see our seed as significant. Always know that you will have enough to help and serve others. If you don't have food, then offer your service(s). You many not have money, but you can give your time and other resources. Do not limit your service to others. Your service helps to provide you with needed encouragement and it helps to take your mind off your problems and concerns. I truly believe God honors our service to others. He sees our service and rewards us for it. So give your time, energy, money, or whatever you have to help others. What you have could very well be your seed, not your harvest. Do not eat it or throw it away. Plant it in the right spot. And if you have a business of some sort, always remember that the seed is greater than the sale.

I have been called crazy for saying that in the past. That is mainly because people did not realize the beauty of the seed or a harvest. Many people look at the harvest of trees and think that is the most significant aspect of the forest. Wise men and women look at the seeds that fall from the tree. One tree is capable of producing many seeds. And one seed is able to produce a tree that ultimately produces more seeds. Your service or product goes a long way when you give it freely as directed. It is like a seed sown in good ground. It takes time for it to grow, but it will grow. Once it grows you will notice the magnificence of the harvest. It never fails that the seed always produces a harvest that is greater than the seed itself. The harvest will always be greater than the seed. I am still using this principle in my life.

This is the sixth book I have self-published. The process was not easy. It took a lot of time and energy, but I ultimately figured it out. I have helped countless people self-publish their books. I have been asked how much would I charge them for my assistance. I have yet to charge anyone. I do not help every person who asks because the demand is just too great. Nevertheless, I help without expecting anything in return. I know my seed will be greater than my sale. Will I continue to offer my self-publishing services for free? Probably not, but I believe my selfless act will return a harvest much greater than what I would receive if I were to charge each person who asked.

My wife and I have had people ask us why we do not sell our sermons. The money could definitely be used. However, the preaching of the truth is not for sale. It is our desire to freely give it. We believe that God will continue to supply us the opportunities and space to preach His word and the mediums to provide it for free. Now, there are certain conferences and retreats that require a significant amount of money to host the events. It is only proper business sense that we charge for those events. But our goal is never to poach the people with an unreasonable amount to make a high profit. Our events are priced in such a way that people can afford them whether they reside in the projects or in a palace. We do our best to remain appealing to all so that none are left out.

It is my heart's desire to plant good seeds in good ground, so I sow willingly and with thanksgiving. I also give as an honor to God. He compels me, so it is my honor and privilege to obey Him. It is your honor and privilege as well. Give yourself and your stuff away to Him and others. It is our privilege and our utmost honor.

I remember being very upset with God one Sunday morning because my car would not start. I was up early for church, and I had every intention of being there. I got in the car to find out that it would not start. I was not sure why. I went back in the house, put my loungewear back on, and got back in the bed. That was it! I did not try anything else. I was just frustrated my car did not start. Fast-forward almost seven years to me riding to an old shed in the middle of a small village in Addis Ababa, Ethiopia. I was headed there to preach. We pulled up to a hungry crowd of people awaiting my arrival. The host stated they had been waiting more than two hours for me to arrive. I was not late. In fact, I was an hour early! The host proceeded to tell me how some people walked an hour or so to get to the location. They did not have proper means to travel. Some who arrived did not have a place to sit so they were forced to stand the entire time. I remember back to my unwillingness to walk or find another option to get me to church so that I could assemble with other believers. My motivation was wrong and I looked at my problems as if they were insurmountable.

One of my favorite preachers, Leonard Ravenhill, told a story about a preacher who traveled from Africa to preach in America. Before he took the pulpit to preach the pastor of the church welcomed the congregation. The pastor said, "Oh, I just want to thank y'all for coming out tonight. I know the weather is cold. It is just so uncomfortable. I just want to thank you from the bottom of my heart for being here." The pastor was ready to rapture the entire congregation at that moment just because they came to church. The guest preacher then came to take the pulpit. With his head bowed low he said, "Yes, I want to thank you all for coming to church tonight. I want to thank you for leaving your warm house to get in your warm car to travel and sit in this warm church on the plush and comfortable pews. Oh! I just want to thank you!" He then proceeded to say, "I looked forward to preach here tonight, but I have to throw up first. You people make me sick." Harsh words, right?

Consider what this preacher said. He told the congregation how many of his friends and family had to walk miles to get to and from church gatherings. He said it was very dangerous seeing that many of them had to walk at night. They had to cross the dangerous landscape where some became lunch for hungry lions. Those who made it passed the lions had to defend themselves from hungry crocodiles who lined the Nile River. Many were helpless when they had to fight off the territorial hippos. They suffered through the weather elements to assemble together. They traveled in difficult hardship because they knew it would be worth it in the end.

Many of us here in America, and other places, do not have that same kind of passionate sacrifice and zeal to deny ourselves and travel the dark roads at night to assemble with other believers. We take our opportunities to gather together for granted. Churches are neatly positioned on every corner of most cities. We have churches everywhere, and it breaks my heart to drive past them and see the doors closed and lights off.

I look forward to the day we are blessed with our own church building. It is my desire for The Gathering Oasis Church, the church I pastor in Atlanta, Georgia, to remain open at all times. We will have prayer and praise going on all day and night. We will host a service each night. If God never sleeps or slumbers, why should the places we assemble to learn, break bread and gather close its doors and have specific times of prayer and worship? What is wrong with us? What have we become?

I continue to remind the people who gather at The Gathering Oasis Church that we have a major responsibility. No one can be lazy. It will require work from everyone, and we all must remain pure for God's precious anointing to flow through us as we serve His people. It breaks my heart that many choose not to assemble just because it rained outside or because there was a little frost on the ground. Our devotion to assemble with other believers is not sure. I have met men and women in other countries who assemble privately because they could be put to death if anyone found out about them.

What has happened to us? We have become a people who are absorbed in self and increasing our worldly comforts. It is ruining us from the inside out. Do not allow for it to ruin you. Open your life and serve others. Give yourself away. Stop focusing on what you do not have and be bold about serving. Do it with thankfulness, gladness, and without expecting anything in return. We all have lack in some area of our life. Do not think you are alone.

Chapter 2

THE STRUGGLE WITH SEXUAL ADDICTION

Sexual addiction is more than a struggle for many; it is an all-out war! It is a daily battle started in our most intimate thoughts and given birth in our actions. It is the offspring of our carnal nature and a complete misuse of our body, which is the temple of the Holy Spirit. Many are attacked throughout the day with thoughts of sex. I recently read an article stating the average male thinks about sex every thirty seconds. I do not know the reality of such a statement, but I do know thoughts about sex can be reoccurring and very dominant. The article stated that men cannot concentrate on the tasks before them because they are weighed down with perverse thoughts. They undress people with their eyes—both male and female. No one is safe from his or her inner battle.

I know that battle so well because I was once an active fighter in it. I would be a lie to say I do not still fight today. The battle is a real one. It is an intense war that has ruined many lives. The foundation of it is pride, which gives birth to lust. Pride is the absolute single source of all sin. By it we exchange the truth of the Word of God for a lie, suppress it in unrighteousness and twist it in perversion until it leads to destruction. The pride I am speaking of is the pride of life. It seals the eyes of understanding, promotes immorality and always favors sin. And we can always tell where the pride of life and lust has been because it leaves behind a trail of perverse actions, shattered hearts and broken homes.

I fully intend for my words in this chapter to be stinging and transparent. You may see yourself in what I write. What is important is that you recognize that you are not alone in your fight with sexual addiction. Freedom is possible through our Lord Jesus Christ and the continuous work of the Holy Spirit within us. He pleads the case for holiness. He convicts us when we are going in a way that is opposite of holiness and purity. He desires that we remain holy, as He is holy. We must yield ourselves to Him and allow Him to finish the work He has begun in us. Let's get started.

I have met men and women who were addicted to sex, as was I. Their heart's desire was to engulf themselves in sexual intercourse with whomever would give them permission to do so. They completely lowered their guard to allow for their emotional and physical fantasies to materialize. I do not necessarily believe they enjoyed the sex as much as they enjoyed the chase—the thrill they got from trying to capture and bring their wildest fantasies to life.

The chase can be exciting and fun because the possibilities are almost endless. Curiosity guides the man or woman to venture into an unknown world to feed his or her intimate desires. Oftentimes, those desires are not discussed publically in fear she or he will be ridiculed or cast away. I have met men who lusted after children, different kinds of women, and different kinds of men. I have also met women with the same desires. Through conversation it becomes apparent they are after something they realize is wrong. They either ignore or challenge what they think is wrong so they can find a way to do what they want. Some sneak away in the dark. Others do their dirtiest of work during the day. They all find a way to do what their heart desires and fulfill their fantasy.

I know that was my case. I hungered after affection, and most times, I did not care where it came from. I desired attention, so I sought it wherever I could find it. I wanted someone to love me; to think of me; to want me. I wanted to feel special; to be held; to be desired. I searched for some kind of affection and relief in pornography—the most superficial form of intimacy. The effects of it were damaging. It caused me to live in a world of sex because everything around me began to remind me of it. I could not watch cartoons without imaging lustful activity between the characters. It caused me to suppress the truth I would hear from the Word of God and live in the shadows because I was too ashamed to let others know about my sin. I could not be "me" because I was ashamed of my private actions. I could not be transparent in conversation with others because I felt like I was the only one struggling. My love for self began to fade away. I did not like looking at myself in the mirror. I knew I was a hypocrite and a coward. I needed help, but I was not willing to reach out and ask for it. It was complete torture.

Pornography is not real or fulfilling. It keeps the person who is engaged in it coming back for more. The satisfaction gained from it is temporary. It is like fireworks—a loud bang and a lot of noise that soon disappears until the next show is performed. The foundation of it is lust, and lust is never satisfied.

Pornography was safe for me because it allowed me to indulge myself in temporary satisfaction without having to give anything substantial. Well, I felt like I was not giving anything substantial. I failed to realize I was lending my most prized possession—my mind. I felt as though it was a safe place to explore my sexuality and fulfill all of my desires without having to commit myself to a real relationship. I did not have to meet anyone's parents, go out on a date, meet friends, or any of the normal realities associated with a relationship. I continued to go back to pornography to indulge in sexual immorality and feed my lustful desires. That was the goal whether I wanted to admit it or not. I did not want conversation. I did not want long walks on the beach. I did not want to be nagged. I was not looking for anything special or lasting. I would love to make it seem like I was fighting against the desire to watch pornography and masturbate, but I would be a liar.

Fighting is an active word. That means one has to be actively engaged in order for him to be fighting. I was not fighting or resisting the temptation; I was lying down and allowing the temptation to trample me under its feet. I was not in a posture to fight, which means I was not stepping on the battlefield with the mindset that I was going to win, or die trying. I was going on the battlefield without any armor on or even an action plan to fight. I would oftentimes make others think I was going to fight. In actuality, I was going fully prepared to be defeated. My armor was not real; my prayers were not heartfelt. I was a phony who was pretending to live a godly life before the congregation while lending myself to the desires of my perverse heart. I was a coward. There you have it. I said it. I was definitely a coward, one who ran away from a fight to hide.

I oftentimes wondered if fighting the sexual temptation was worth it. I have found that giving in to my lustful desires over and over again created a mindset that did not desire to fight. Why fight when it seems so much easier to cave in to the sensual desires that vexed my heart? I would find myself wanting to pour out my heart to those I met and let them in to my inner struggles. But I would only get so far after realizing I did not really trust they could help me. I was constantly told I should run to Jesus— the only one who could help me. Unfortunately, I did not know what that meant. I did not understand the depth of faith involved in the deliverance power of Jesus I desperately needed. It took a faith so deep that it would not bend or break when it was tried. I did not realize it took time to truly trust and believe in the lordship and saving power of Jesus.

I got tired of what I referred to as "church sayings." These are sayings like: "run to Jesus," "call on Him when you need Him," or "let Him in you." I had no clue what it meant to run to Jesus. I would oftentimes question why I had to run to Him seeing that He is sitting at the right hand of the Father. Am I supposed to run to the throne? Where is the throne? I will never forget a gentleman telling me to run to the throne of God right after I confessed the Lord Jesus. I left that place so confused because I did not have a clue where the throne was located. I did not know what it meant. Although it sounds nice, it provides no real direction to the infant believer.

And I did not know how to call on Jesus or to let Him in me. The idea of letting Him in me was a little far-fetched to me. I could not grasp the idea that He wanted to live in me. The sayings

I received, and later gave out to others, did not make any sense to me because my faith was so young. I began to grow bitter against the church-at-large because of its culture of throwing out sayings I did not feel they really understood themselves. It made me think that if I really wanted change, I probably would not get it from the church.

I believe true healing came from my eyes being opened to the truth. This means I was able to recognize my sinful actions for what they were. God allowed me to see the wrong of my ways. It was clear that my actions were sinful. I was fully convicted, and conviction brings repentance. That means I fully turned away from my wrongdoing. I needed to turn away from it.

Repentance is more than just being sorry for my actions. It means I recognize my sin and I am turning away from it for good. Repentance is not just saying, "I am sorry." It is more than just being remorseful because you got caught in the sinful act. For example, I had someone catch me one night while I was purchasing pornographic movies from an adult novelty store. I had a fake ID at the time that allowed me to get into the store. I drove over an hour away from my home to go there. Unfortunately, it did not matter. There was someone in the same shopping center who I knew from high school. The person wanted to make sure I saw him. "Cornelius! What are you doing?" His question was hard-hitting because he could see my hypocrisy. I was trying to live one way in front of my classmates while living another way privately. Many would just say that my actions were none of his business. However, I was a leader in high school. Many chose to follow me. My actions were leading them in a direction that was not right. He called me out about it in front of the store.

Now, you must know that his life was not white as snow, but he made some good points. I was very remorseful for my actions, but that remorse did not lead to repentance. I got in my car, and he watched me drive off. I parked in the lot about a half a mile down the road. I waited there about thirty minutes then drove back to the adult novelty store. I went in, got what I wanted, and left. The remorse was short-lived. I have done that multiple times. I felt bad for my actions, but that was not enough to bring true repentance. And it is only through real repentance that we realize the wrong of our ways and make lasting changes.

I also had to learn the importance of discipline. I had to act out on my faith. I believed I was healed and delivered from many of my sin-sick desires so I needed to live my life accordingly. That means I could no longer entertain the same people who encouraged sinful behavior. I had to cut off all communication with anyone who threatened my peace and placed my desire for holiness in danger. I had to cut off the contact that helped to supply me with the pornography and adult-friendly websites. I had to deny temptation each and every time it came seeking to trap me in a pit of sin. I had to do simple things like place my laptop in a room where everyone could see me. I knew, as we all know, that it is more difficult to commit any act of outward sexual sin while others are around. I had to replace my desire to watch pornographic films with an act that would be uplifting to my soul and eternity—prayer. I needed to really get serious about my life and live as if my deliverance was sure and real. Have I messed up? Of course. Will I stay down after sinning? Absolutely not. Will I continue to habitually practice the sin? No, I will not. I am proud to say that I have not turned back to it though. That is true freedom. It is truly freeing.

I was oftentimes ruined after I had failed and fallen back into the sin I told myself I would never go back to. The sting of defeat haunted me over and over again. It haunted me so much that I did not want to fight it any longer. I would tell myself that I would not do it anymore. My so-called remorse was short-lived. I told myself that the late night rendezvous were over, but I found myself right back in that same position over and over again. Pretty soon, I found myself in lasciviousness. I knew I was chasing something. I was chasing the climax I felt the first time I experienced my sinful desires being fulfilled. I wanted to recreate that moment I first felt the exhilarating feeling after engaging in some kind of sexual act. I knew the chase was wrong. But that did not stop me. I sat there on the front row in a church service that accommodated almost 10,000 people a week. I sat there willing to lift my hands and put on the image of holiness fully knowing that I was filled with perversion. I was learning how to perfect the outward image while allowing my heart to remain polluted with the lusts of the world. I was being taunted by voices even while I sat in the church service. I would rush home just so I could find a quiet place to watch sinful filth. I would proclaim my love, allegiance, and adoration for God while continuing to engage in all the things He hates.

My heart grew cold and continued to harden because I wanted desperately to find relief and have a safe place I could discuss my sexual escapades. Sadly, I found my greatest relief outside of the church walls! Can you believe that? I found more transparency with those who were not in the church than I did with those who were inside of it. This is mainly because many on the inside were content with living a lie and others were trying to perfect the life of perfection. Many wanted so desperately to be and appear faultless that they could no longer relate to the reality we all share, which is we are all fallen men and women who are capable of failing over and over again. The only hope we have is in the perfected work of Jesus Christ. We should be thankful for grace and mercy. However, this does not mean we should not pursue holiness and perfection in this life we live. It should be an active pursuit. It must never become a life of trying to hide your sin and pretending like you have it all together. I know that life. It is a lonely one. I know it because I was perfecting it.

My sexual addictions led me down a dark road. My goal is to show you that you are not alone. The sexual frustration you have is real. I know because I have felt it. However, you do not have to live in it. Ask God to fully open your eyes to the truth so you are able to see the wrong of your ways, and ask Him to give you strength so you can turn away from the sin once and for all. It is time for you to stop.

Finally, what really helped to deliver me was something I had never heard before in all my years of being churched—a convicting sermon on the fear of God. I write more about it in the next two chapters. The reverence and esteem I have for Him keeps me out of sin. It keeps me walking in the Spirit so I do not fulfill the desires of my flesh. It has kept me and brought a reality to my sinful situation that I did not understand before. Keep reading to see how that particular sermon changed my life.

Chapter 3

IN THE MIDST OF THE ASSEMBLY

There I sat in the midst of the assembly. There were people all around me but I felt like I was alone. Have you ever felt that way? I sat there in the midst of the assembly broken, dejected, lost, and afraid. Could I find some measure of solace for my pain and discomfort? I would hope so. But where could I go to find comfort and peace? Who could I fully trust to rely and lean on? Who could I pour my heart out to? I needed answers. I needed a solution. I needed help as I sat in the midst of other believers.

Who made up the assembly? I would assume there were professionals of all fields, people from all tax brackets, married folks, singles, intellectuals, and those from different cultures. The assembly was old and young. Men and women were of all heights and sizes. Some were more financially secure than others. Some were clothed in the finest clothing money could buy. Others wore whatever their pockets could afford. The assembly was diverse and extremely special. I am sure many had an educated opinion on what they believed I could do to ease my depression. Although the assembly was large in number, I still felt like I was alone to deal with my problems.

There I sat in the middle of the assembly in silent protest.

This is where I expressed strong disapproval without saying a word. Have you ever heard of the story about little Johnny? He was told to sit in the corner because he was so active. As he sat in the corner, he looked at his mom and said, "I may be sitting down in the corner, but I am standing up inside!" That is a type of silent protest—a protest that is without words but filled with action. It is an act of defiance. I am sure you have probably done the same thing. I was protesting the thought that I needed to seek help in those around me. But the truth is, the reason I was protesting was because I felt like everyone was a hypocrite and a fraud. I felt like they were self-righteous bigots set out on exposing my weaknesses to make themselves look better or choosing to manipulate my vulnerabilities and exploit my shame.

If I am honest, I had every opportunity to talk to someone and bear my burdens with others. I could easily confess my issues and faults with those around me, but I was afraid. I feared the image I had created would be tarnished or ruined if I was fully exposed. I feared the judgment would be too severe if the evidence were made public. Have you ever had a trial by public opinion? It is torturous! The public does not have a law degree, and they do not qualify their evidence. They judge based on their feelings, and the judgment can be harsh. I did not want to experience it again. I felt like the consequences of the sinful actions I tried to keep hidden would be too much to bear. I did not feel like others would relate or understand my instability. I was a man drunk on sin and saturated in foolishness. I had knowledge of what I needed to do, but I did not want to do it. I was fighting an inner battle—a war between two extremes. I also felt like I was the only one suffering.

How do I suffer in silence while others are all around me who are supposed to help? These are supposed to be my Christian brothers and sisters. Where are the good Samaritans who see their fallen brother and are willing to provide assistance? Where are they? What happened to the church in that sense? Have we become so focused on ourselves that we have refused to concern ourselves with the needs and ailments of others?

Do you understand the magnitude of what it means to be in the midst of the assembly of believers? It is different from dancing in the club, shooting drugs up my arm in the alley, or drinking with the drunks from the bar. Unfortunately, many of those around me in the assembly also were the ones in the bar, in the alley, and in the club. And they were not there to preach repentance and salvation through Jesus. They were there to partake of all the perverse fruit the environment had to offer. But the assembly of believers should be a safe place; an inviting place; a forgiving place. It should not be a place of hiding and rejection. However, it was all around me.

It seemed like the lives of those around me were perfect. Some were moving on in their careers. Others were getting engaged, married, and having children. Some were dressed in the finest clothes money could buy. And there I was lonely and in despair while giving the appearance of success and happiness. I put on my smile every morning like I put on my clothes. It was part of my attire. I even started buying into the hype of "faking it until I made it." It is the idea that I could fake the actions until I finally got what I was after. I would have to continue putting on the appearance of success until it finally materialized. Unfortunately, I became a professional faker because I continued to practice the art of faking it. Never forget that you will perfect whatever you practice. If you practice faking it, do not be surprised when you begin to perfect it.

I wanted desperately to cry out and ask for help. But again, who could I turn to in my moment of weakness? It seemed like none of my friendships afforded me the opportunity to remove the masks I wore or to reveal my true self. The assembly served as the grave where I was being buried while others stood by. Did anyone notice my decay? Could they not smell the stench of sin radiating off me? Could they not see the hopelessness in my eyes? Were they blind to my sinful actions? Had they turned a deaf ear to my cries of help? Should I place that responsibility on them? All I wanted were brothers who would keep me, challenge me, and shame my wrongdoing. Anything. Something. I wanted help. I needed help. I was desperate for help. But my desire for help did not lead to repentance. I did not reach out for assistance either. My desire for help was silent. My cries were silent. My tears were shed silently. And my heart was hardening more and more. I was in a very dangerous place.

While in the midst of the assembly, I would gaze upon the preacher as he preached with passion and force about the promises of God. I sat there in amazement as he presented the sermon in such a way that it demanded my full attention. Even though I listened, I did not fully take in all he was saying. I was hesitant—very hesitant. I began to think his tailored suits, diamond-studded ring, and beautifully arranged pulpit is all a front. I felt like he hides behind those things. I began to rationalize in my head why I should not hear what he had to say. I watched as congregants in the assembly stood to their feet to applaud him for what he said. I looked at them from the corner of my eye. I only imagined the lives they lived and the secrets lurking in their closet. I presumed the front row was filled with the holier-than-thous—those who exchanged persecution for prosperity and brokenness for beauty. They were poised and polished as if it was all rehearsed. In fact, I remember seeing the same faces the last week and the week before and the week before. They put on the same show over and over again.

My mind conjured up many thoughts about those in the assembly to the point I felt like I was the only one suffering in silence. Little did I know, I was not alone. The front row looked successful and full of happiness, but many of them put on their smile like they put on their clothes just like me. The couple on the end just filed for bankruptcy for the second time after another failed attempt at starting a business. Another couple was on the brink of divorce. The gentleman to my immediate left was near foreclosure on his home and about to have his car repossessed. Hardship was all around but the goal of appearing perfect was too important for them. It could have been they did not have a safe place to pour our their heart, confess their hardship, and ask for help. Instead they attempted to live under a false sense of reality—a reality that suppresses instead of confesses. I learned a valuable lesson while suffering in the midst of the assembly: there is just as much mess in the mansion as there is pain the projects.

I absolutely loathe the popular message found in the churches of our day that promotes Christianity as if it were another piece of the American Dream. Many American "preachers" attempt to sell that dream across the pond to other countries. Unfortunately, some have taken to the message and started to drink it down like water. There is nothing pure about it. It is presented in such a way that Jesus is just the missing element to reach financial success and healing. They offer Him as a promise to the lost who desire and hunger for worldly success. He ceases from being Lord in their teachings; He becomes brother and friend. Please understand that I do understand the friendship we share with our Lord; however, even He described His friends as those who follow His commands. The message presented by the health and wealth preachers of our day comes with false hope. They seek to accommodate the masses and make them comfortable in their selfish desires. They highlight a dangerous lie—that God desires everyone to be rich, comfortable, and happy. They fail to mention the countless number of Christians who are persecuted daily having their heads severed from their bodies, some dipped in boiling oil while still alive, and others tarred and set on fire. They do not mention their comfort, happiness, or riches. I am sure it is not comfortable to have a dull blade run around your neck as the agitator severs your head from your body. I am sure there is no happiness found in being pushed into a church building while agitators set the whole place ablaze. I am sure their mind is not set on worldly riches when they are being sentenced to die the worst kinds of deaths because of their allegiance to our Lord. They understand that happiness is only a feeling.

True believers are not in search of happiness; they are in search of joy, which is found in Jesus alone. Our faith in Him and the comforting presence of the Holy Spirit brings great joy to our heart. Happiness is based on how we feel; joy is based on what we know. Having a revealed knowledge of the truth and understanding the saving grace of our God gives us a great assurance. That is the joy we seek. True comfort is not in worldly riches or selfish attainment of worldly success. In fact, true success is obeying God in all things. That is true success. Some may ask, "Cornelius, would you say that persecution for the obedient believer is success?" Absolutely! Jesus stood on the mount and told all who gathered that those who are persecuted are blessed. They are truly blessed. Big houses and fancy cars do not make anyone blessed. True believers find riches in the presence of God. They see riches as obedience even when it hurts and is not comfortable.

I have sat in the midst of an assembly that preached a twisted message of hope. It did nothing more than make my heart sick. I would sit there week after week hoping and praying for God to make a car fall from the sky just because I gave a few dollars in the offering. I did not give because I loved God; I gave because I wanted Him to do something for me. My motivation was wrong and ill intended. My heart grew sick as so many do within today's assembly. Many have wandered from the faith because of a heavy heart. They blame God for their unhappiness, comfort, and lack of earthly riches because they believe, or have been taught, they should receive them. He goes from being their Heavenly Father to their sugar daddy. This is a horrible reality within many of our assemblies today. The false hope in many of these messages keeps people from being transparent. Instead of recognizing and embracing persecution and the tests of life as a working out of our endurance they hide behind a veil of false reality. Their false reality matches the false message they are taught. This false message appeals to our pleasures and brings tolerance to ungodliness. The teachers of this message do not seek to offend anyone. They make it comfortable for others who live a different religion to sit in the midst of the assembly without any conviction at all.

Let's take a look and see what we can learn about becoming wise to the subtle influence of the enemy in the church. Let's see what could happen if these walls could talk.

Chapter 4

IF THESE WALLS COULD TALK

If the walls in our house, office, or coffee shop could talk, I only wonder what they would say. I know the walls in my house would have a lot to say. They would reveal a truth about me that is kept away from the public.

The walls in our life represent privacy. It is common for rooms in a house to be separated by walls. The walls provide a sense of security and intimacy. There is usually a door—which is capable of being locked—to ensure control over when and who is allowed to enter. The walls in our lives hide many things, and many think what is hidden is out of God's sight. However, they quickly learn that what is hidden from man is not hidden from God.

Could you imagine what your walls would say if they could talk? Would they unearth family secrets that could rock the lives of everyone who hears them? Would they tell a story of abuse, both physical and emotional? What would they say? Would they tell of your late night rendezvous? Would they uncover the very things you have been trying to hide? Would they tell the story of your suicide attempts and sensual moments of pleasure in front of a computer as you viewed strangers having sex with one another? What would they say?

Growing up, I lived with the idea that every family was normal besides mine. I saw a great deal of dysfunction and abuse—mostly mental. Alcohol became my worst enemy because I felt like it destroyed my father, which eventually ruined my family. The destruction of the head brings complete ruin to the rest of the body. It caused many arguments in my household. It placed a heavy strain on our family for years. I will never forget the horrible shouting matches held between my parents because of my father's late night rendezvous with alcohol. He would go to his grandmother's house, a place where alcohol was served throughout the day and night, and get drunk with his family and friends. It was common for him to get drunk and drive. I recall never knowing what the next phone call to our home would entail. We got so many emergency phone calls from rescue personnel who found a completely totaled car, which was registered in my father's name, but no one would be inside of it. My father managed to escape the grasp of death many times. I imagine he probably wished he had stayed in the wreckage because the fight that awaited him at home was probably more than what he bargained for. I had many sleepless nights where I did not know if my father was alive, if he was going to be drunk, or if I would have to hear the arguing.

I found a little peace of heaven in my room. I did not have doors I could shut seeing that my room also served as a hallway. I would place a sheet in front of the hallway entrance to give myself a little privacy. It would not keep out the arguments, but it gave me the feeling that I was alone and safe. I would bury my head in my pillow and cry myself to sleep. I spent many nights wishing and praying I was not alive. I had somehow bought the lie that I was probably the problem and everyone would be better if I was dead.

The walls to my old room could tell a very deep and intimate story of pain and self-hatred. They would tell a story of a boy battling a private sexual battle and a hateful desire deep in his heart because every time he looked at himself in the mirror he hated the way he looked. Those were the walls that witnessed my childhood—or lack thereof. Those were the walls that witnessed my insecurities being birthed and developed. Those were walls that watched me as I tried to watch X-rated material late at night after my parents went to bed. Those walls watched as I tried to act out the sex scenes I watched on television with the girls who came over to our home. Those walls listened as I began using every curse word I heard around me. It was also between those walls that I tried to forget everything that ever happened to me.

A family that lived a little ways from us had their own share of problems. No one could really tell it from the outside looking in. They seemed like your "perfect" family. The parents seemed to have great jobs; the children seemed to be at the top of their classes respectfully. Their house was absolutely beautiful. It was one of the largest homes I had ever seen. The image they gave off to everyone was very believable. It was not until I was about to move to Georgia in 2000 that the truth started to come out about them. What looked like a perfect marriage was really a great stage performance. The husband and wife did not even sleep in the same bed, or room for that matter. Being that they were so far apart one could only imagine they did not share any intimacy. They only wanted to stay together for the wellbeing of their children. They ended up going to the courts to seek a divorce the day after the last child moved out. They were tired of the act.

Many rumors began to swirl around town about them but nothing was ever substantiated. I was finally able to speak with one of the children, which also happened to be an old classmate of mine. It was there she divulged the hidden secrets of infidelity, alcoholism, drugs, and hatred. The stress from the job sent the husband and father into the arms of alcohol and drugs. His addiction led him to some horrible decisions. The wife and mother sought affection and intimacy, so she ran to obtain it in the arms of another man. After it became known, violence erupted and a deep bed of anger was created in both of their hearts. God was nowhere in the middle of it. The daughters— hungry for affection, affirmation, and identity—began chasing boys and anything that could curb their dangerous desire for acceptance. After many abortions, failed suicide attempts, and early morning emergency runs to have alcohol pumped from their stomachs, they were still searching for answers and dealing with the dysfunction of their childhood and household. One of the main things that stuck out in her confession was the difficulty in trying to keep the secret and live a lie.

Are you like my old classmate? Are you trying to cope and live with the dysfunction? I am constantly reminded that I am a very important part of our family's unit. If I am absent emotionally or physically, it could cause my wife and son to rebel and seek what they feel they need in other areas. Those different ways to cope could lead to serious problems, even death. Most times, we do not think of the effect of emotional absence. Our society places a greater significance on physical absence.

I remember hearing a motivational speaker give an hour-long message about his father being absent in his life. He spoke about the pain he felt in his heart. It was troubling to hear. However, I could not help but think about my own pain and struggles. I felt like I could empathize with him even though my father was present. Yes, I saw him daily. He was a very present figure in our home. Unfortunately, he was silent. I write in-depth about his silence and how much it affected me in my book, *So, You Want to be a Man?* I encourage you to get a copy and read through it. I remember going up to the speaker after he was done and telling him how much I enjoyed his speech. I remember walking back to my seat and gripping my shirt. I began to feel a lot of different emotions. I was angry and I wanted to cry. I was upset because I felt like I would have preferred to have never known my father than to have known and lived with him without any emotional connection at all.

I am sure your walls could speak at length about all they have witnessed. I want you to do something that I know will not be easy. I want you to break down the walls, figuratively speaking. I do not want you to literally go around your house breaking down walls. I want you to properly identify the walls in your life that you are using to shield your secrets. It is time to break them down. I am not sure if you have ever seen walls torn down, but it is quite a spectacle. Imagine a room with a wall through the center of it. The wall is purposed to separate the two rooms. There is usually a door that allows access between the two spaces. The wall allows for some privacy between the rooms. This allows for the person on one side to stay hidden and practice their heart's desires without being seen by those on the other side of the wall.

I have lived in a condo before where my wife and I had to listen as the couple living next door to us argued loudly. We could hear them through the walls. We did not see them with our eyes, but we knew they were arguing. The wall kept their actions hidden even though we could hear things being thrown around the room and hitting the wall. Tearing down the wall makes the room completely open. It removes the one-way entrance through the door and eliminates the privacy. It places everything out in the open to be seen by all. I know the idea of full exposure is scary. People run away from the exposure so their deeds will not be plain to see. You must know that exposing your actions brings accountability.

The very thought of exposing everything and tearing down the walls you have created in your life could seem like more than what you can handle. I do not know what you are trying to hide behind them, but I can tell you that it is not worth it. Do not perfect living a lie. Are you trying to hide your secret compulsion for the same-sex? Is it driving you into secret meetings and outings with people you would not normally meet in public or around your closest friends? Do not become perfect at living a lie. Tear down the walls you have created. Tear down the walls around your family secrets and problems. Go ahead and bury all those skeletons from your closet. Forgive those who betrayed, molested, haunted, mistreated, or terrorized you. Let it go! Forgive them as the Father has forgiven you through the sacrifice of Jesus Christ. I realize it is a sense of betrayal to discuss family problems with anyone outside of the family and the house. Many see it as a violation of the family's trust. I am asking you to look beyond that idea and confess what has happened with mature, Spirit-filled counselors, your pastor or church elders. Pour out your heart to God. You maybe thinking why is it important to tell God what happened if He already knows. Well, confession is an act of faith, and God is pleased by our faith. It is better to release and confess what you are holding in instead of continuing to try to hide it away. The idea that you will betray your family by divulging secrets can be difficult for you and the people involved. I have seen families fall apart because secrets of incest and rape were revealed. Those who commit the sins are oftentimes ashamed of their transgressions and prefer for them to stay hidden. Do not live in the shadows any longer. Speak with a Spirit-filled counselor, your pastor, church elder, or someone who is mature, willing and able to advise you. I strongly advise you to be cautious with the information you share. It is a very delicate process. Use wisdom and discernment. Confess to God first in prayer. Healing is a process we enter into when we accept that something is wrong. God is able to heal. We just have to want to be healed for God's power to be experienced. Tear down the walls through confession of your sins and submission to Christ. You are not alone.

Chapter 5

I'M NOT HAPPY

I will never forget the day my wife looked at me with tears in her eyes and said, "I'm not happy." Those words followed a very intense and hurtful argument. We both said some really mean things about one another. We hit below the belt with our words, and I know what I said hurt her. I used my tongue as a weapon of mass destruction like I had in the past. I know because her declaration of unhappiness really hurt me. I did not know how to verbalize the hurt. I could not just come out and cry the tears I could feel welling up inside. It was like she shot a cannon ball at my heart. The cannon hit the target, and my heart was shattered to pieces. Nevertheless, I am glad she said it because it gave us an opportunity to evaluate our marriage and our lives. It also gave me the opportunity to ask myself the question I feared answering: "Am I happy?" I knew my answer would be a resounding "NO!"

Like many newly married folk, I was trying to buy into the disillusionment of marriage perfection. I wanted to believe I was a great husband, a consistent provider, a passionate lover, and a respected leader. The honest truth was that I did not live up to those lofty expectations. I was soaring below them. I realized my foolish ways in my marriage and all the opportunities I missed to provide security to my wife. I asked her to assess me as her husband. I did not want to live in the lie any longer. I did not want to commit a sin of omission. Sadly, I knew what she was going to say. I knew the things I was not doing. The Holy Spirit would convict me to do them, but I would quench Him. I would push away His guidance so I could do my own thing. I knew what to do; I just would not do it.

All those missed opportunities were starting to catch up to me. I could no longer ignore them. It was like I was face-to-face with a brick wall that was built out of my failed opportunities and carelessness. I could not blame it on anyone but myself. It was not the devil. It was not my wife. I could not blame it on my responsibilities. It was time to look at myself. That was a real knock away at my pride. Humility sees the wrong and is willing to address it; pride ignores the wrong and places the burden on others. I had to put my money were my mouth was and lead by example. It was time to face reality.

My wife was prepared to assess me as a husband, and I greatly feared her assessment. I knew there were many areas I lacked, and I knew all the improvements I needed to make. Unfortunately and honestly, I just did not want to make them. I heard what she had to say, and it really hit me like a sack of bricks. I needed to hear it. I needed to be humbled and shown the truth. In fact, I felt better after she said what she said. She showed her love for me. I believe true love is honest, and she was totally honest with me.

While thinking about what she said, I came to the conclusion that I was unhappy with my marriage and I did not "like" the woman I married. I was basing my happiness on what

I liked, not what I needed. Like a child, I focused on what I liked. I had to mature. The problem with likes is they can and often do change. What I liked as a child is different from what I like as an adult. I had to mature beyond my ability to see the things I liked. I know that statement stings to read especially in this society we live in today. Like so many in the world, I hid my dislikes under the mask of perfection and a good image. I did not want my wife to think I saw any flaws in her. I would suppress my true feelings without knowing that I was creating a bigger problem that I would have to deal with later on. Did I think my wife was the problem? Yes, partly. However, I knew the larger part of the problem was with me. Many of things I disliked in her were things I disliked about myself. As I stated earlier, I knew many of the things I needed to change to make our marriage better, but I did not want to change them. My unwillingness to change them was a passive-aggressive attempt at telling her I did not respect her enough to change. Was I wrong? Absolutely.

What about love, Cornelius? What about loving your wife as Christ loves the Church? What about sacrificing yourself for her? What about the deep devotion you should have for your wife? What about all those things? Don't you preach them? Those questions haunted me for a while after I got married. I knew my actions were wrong, but like I said I did not want to change them. I knew I should never allow the sun to go down without making peace with my wife, but I went to sleep anyway. I did not care if she stayed up all night or not. Her feelings did not matter to me in that moment. I knew all the things I preached, but I was not man enough to listen to the words I spoke. Like a coward, I hide behind a false image of masculinity and tried to make it seem like everything was her fault. I quickly got to the point where I realized that I was preaching sermons even I could not obey. I also realized in that moment that many preachers choose to soften the tone of holiness—as if they have that right—because of their unwillingness to mature above their insecurities.

I sat at that crossroad for some time, contemplating whether I would become a preacher who needed to soften his tone and preach a coward's message of perverted grace and mercy so I could feel comfortable in my sin or embrace the perfect work of the Holy Spirit within me so I could be truly changed. That crossroad was a lonely place. I truly felt like I was alone. I was fighting the urge to harden and grow cold against my wife. I did not know how to be a husband. I did not get a tutorial on it. None of the classes I took in school focused on marriage. I felt like a fish out of water. But the moment of truth was before me. Would I change or continue living like a stubborn, foolish man? It was time to change.

Our conversation was fruitful. My wife was able to share what was on her heart, and I was able to share what was on mine. She really listened to me, and I listened to her. I can write these words now and boldly proclaim that my wife and I have a great relationship. Do we have problems and disagreements here and there? Of course; however, they are not as frequent as it was before. We both had deep hurts and resentments we brought into the marriage. We needed healing, and we found it through confession and submission to the work of the Holy Spirit within our marriage and to each other. We prayed together and we could feel the pain and stress lift off our shoulders. We grew closer that night. Our marriage has been great since that day. God really healed us.

As I stated, I was beginning to buy the idea of marriage perfection. I felt like other people's marriage was perfect. Like social media, we have the tendency to give the highlight reel of our perfections and strengths. Very rarely do you see someone posting or bragging about his or her weaknesses or imperfections. Most families teach that weaknesses and issues are best not discussed or broadcast in public. They teach it is best to leave private matters private. And I agree with that principle in many ways. However, I do not believe issues, imperfections, and weaknesses should be ignored and swept under the rug. They must be confessed and dealt with properly. We must learn the duty of confessing our faults one with another. There is great freedom in confession, but we will never know it because many do not ever confess.

I have read many books on marriage, but I hardly ever finish them. I usually get to the third chapter and almost sling the book across the room because I do not believe I can live up to the perfect image that is written about in the book. I read many of the books and I grow fearful because I doubt my marriage would last or that we would be that perfect. My fear was there mostly because I felt like I was the only person feeling that way. I did not stop to consider or even realize that many of the authors of those books were just as imperfect as I.

Please do not get me wrong. I love a good love story and fairy tale ending, but I love transparency and honesty a lot more. I want to know that someone was going through the struggle and came out of it. I want to know I was not the only husband who did not like his wife and regretted getting married. I remember looking at my wife after a very intense argument and telling her, "I should not have married you. I married too young." I freely admit I was hurt, and I was trying to hurt her. My words were immature. But there was some truth to those words. I really felt that way. I felt like I did not want to be with her any longer as my wife. I wanted to have my "freedom" back. I wanted to go and come as I pleased. I wanted to do whatever I wanted to do. Eat whatever I wanted to eat. Go wherever I wanted to go. And so on. I wanted to reset my single life back to where I would sit in my house alone with all the lights off and do absolutely nothing. That is what I wanted. I wanted to be selfish and uncaring. I remember the days I could just enjoy my own pleasures without having to consider anyone else. Marriage took those days away from me, and I was too immature to see that I gained something much more valuable—a wife, manifested favor from God. She was not presented to be my handicap; she was presented to be my helpmeet; my wife; my crown. I had to learn that truth.

The process of learning it is not an easy one. Her words— "I'm not happy!"—really stung. I greatly feared that she was not happy, but I did not want her to admit it. My worst nightmare had come true. To make matters worse, my next response was, "Well, I guess this is it. We should just get a divorce." I was ready to throw in the towel because I was hurt from her honesty. Her admission of unhappiness was not meant to be my cue to run. I could not make it a habit to run each time things became difficult. I had to learn to stay and fight for what I treasured, and I had to learn the value of treasuring my wife enough to fight for her, not with her.

My wife and I spent the next twelve hours not speaking

with each other. I felt like I needed some time to process and digest her statement. After we started speaking again, I asked her the other question I dreaded asking, "What can I do to make you happy?" I knew that is a loaded question, and I knew the answer is going to be loaded as well. I had to ask it though. I had to confront my own insecurities and immaturity. I had to seek the answers. I also had to be sure to use wisdom to dissect from her answer what I could do and what the Spirit of God would need to do in her.

Certain things like being more affectionate and not as demanding were tasks I could perform. And those were some things she requested from me. However, I knew there were some things I could not solve or do to make her happy simply because those things were birthed from her insecurity. She would have to be strengthened by a greater force of power—the Holy Spirit. Our conversation about happiness and expectations lasted for a couple of hours, and we are better because of it.

My wife and I had the honor and pleasure of hosting our first marriage retreat in 2014. I stood before a room of about 50 men and said the words I am sure none of them wanted to hear. I said, "Guys, you have to ask your wife if she is happy. If she is not, you need to discuss with her why she is not and come up with solutions." Like me, they had to place their ego aside and listen for the betterment of their marriage. Some of the men were not in fear at all about the assignment. They accepted it with joy. Some of the men gave me the death stare after I finished. They knew they were about to walk right into a snake pit, but they knew they had to do it.

While I was asking the men to ask the question to their

wife, my wife was teaching the women how to stop being so critical and quarrelsome. She was teaching about the beauty of being compassionate, caring, patient, and loving towards their husband. The goal was to get the husband and wife together so they could have real discussions without any prejudices whatsoever. I know firsthand what it feels like to live in the house and be married to someone you do not like or want to be around. Many of the men in that room were living in total discomfort. They were so far removed from the emotional stability of their home. Some of them had not taken the pulse of their family in years. Confronting the issues and confessing the problems would definitely bring rocky waters, but I had to assure them that the storm does not last always. Peace will restore the calmness of the sea, and everything will calm down. Honesty does not always feel good, but it is vital to the health of a relationship.

It is my prayer that you do not continue living in a dishonest house. My wife and I had to confront another issue in our marriage shortly after her declaration of unhappiness. We had to realize that our dislike for one another made us put on a show for others. It was an act where we did not say two words to one another in the car but somehow seemed like we were best friends once we got in front of others. It was a show, and neither of us were good actors. So the show did not last long. We quickly agreed to be honest and authentic with one another and not play leading roles in a fake story.

I have met single women who carried themselves well but were pain-stricken within because they were lonely and unhappy. My wife and I hosted a singles retreat in 2014 and we had a plethora of unhappy singles there. Many of them confessed to wanting a husband. They felt like their singleness was a sentence of loneliness and pain. They did not find joy in being single. They felt like being alone was a bad thing. In fact, it can be the exact opposite. Being alone allows you to identify your position. Being lonely is an emotion. Both can change, but only one has a negative connotation.

I encourage you to get real and confront the issues before you. Ask yourself and whomever else the hard questions. If you are single, I recommend you tuck what you have read in the back of your mind and remember it when you are married. It will come in handy for you. Finally, I encourage you to be transparent. Do not live behind a mask. Come out of hiding. You are not alone!

Chapter 6

GREENER GRASS ON THE OTHER SIDE

Have you ever thought about what your life would look like if you were someone else? I know many would not admit they actually think about it, but I will be free enough to admit it. For years, I felt like my life would be perfect if I was born in a different family, looked a different way, or even had more money. I felt this way before coming to Christ, of course. Nevertheless, the feeling was constant and nagging. I could not shake it. It drove me to overeat and be very jealous about the lives I saw others living. Unfortunately for me, the life I saw others live on the outside was only the image they wanted me to see. Many of them were hiding some deeply rooted secrets.

I remember a young man who I envied. We will call him Bill. The envy spewed over to the point of jealousy. I saw how his dad loved being around him and enjoyed taking him places. I would hear about his outings with his father and the many things he would get because he desired them. You have to understand that my mind was wrapped up in the wrong things. I was about eleven years old at the time. Seeing this guy at school and hearing more of his stories about him and his father would make me nauseous. I saw how he got everything he wanted. He was a star on the football field. The ladies adored him. Bill's mother seemed very happy and joyous with him all the time. They lived in a gorgeous home. It looked like he got everything he wanted. I could not find much wrong with his life until everything in his life took a drastic turn for the worse.

I will never forget answering our house phone ringing one evening—cell phones were not really available in my home at that time. Another friend who attended school with both of us was on the phone. He began to ask me if I had spoken to our mutual friend, Bill. After what seemed like forever, he stopped crying long enough to tell me that Bill's father had committed suicide. I was taken aback. I did not believe it. I remember all the stories Bill told about his father and the life they lived. It would seem that everything was absolutely perfect. It was so perfect in my eyes that I wanted to trade places with him. I wanted his life, but I was grossly unaware of what that entailed.

It would later come out that his family was extremely broken—like most families. His father had his personal demons he was trying to fight. Bill's mother and father did not have the best relationship behind closed doors. Bill's father tried to make up his inability to connect with his son emotionally by taking him on nice trips and outings. I did not realize that Bill and his father did not communicate much on those trips or that the father would leave Bill alone for hours while we went away to try to silence the demons who tormented him in his head. The picture seemed perfect on the outside. It seemed attainable. It seemed reasonable. It was so glossy and beautifully presented that I wanted it for myself. Well, let me be honest. I wanted Bill's life. I wanted it until I finally began to see how it really was. Then I did not want it any longer.

We all have moments where we think having someone else's life would give us the advantage. We think having someone else's body would make people like us more. We begin to see flaws in ourselves when we compare ourselves to others. In fact, comparing your life to someone else's life belittles everything you have, everything you are, and everything God has made you to be. I had to learn this great truth.

I had to realize that the grass is not greener on the other side. It is best not to look on the other side of the fence and compare your grass to someone else's. Each time I tried to compare my grass to someone else's, I failed to realize their grass was oftentimes fake. I was intoxicated with envy and jealousy. I could not see the grass clearly. I would skip over the irregularities because I was so focused on acquiring what they had instead of being thankful for what I was given. I write a lot about my life in this book and others I have written. It is evident I did not have a perfect upbringing, but who does? Each test and trial in our life prepares us for something new. It is like weights. Each pull, push, and strain provides resistance for our muscles, and resistance helps build strength and endurance.

I have met some amazing people in my life who have accomplished some amazing things. I cannot think of one of them who had a perfect life. I know a few of them who grew up with a lot of money. I mean they had a lot of money, but one of them also had an alcoholic father and a bipolar mother. Another person I knew had a deranged sibling and very poor health growing up. Both of them gave off the impression their life was perfect. They were showing that fake grass on their side. It took a deep look at their lives to see that the image on the outside was not necessarily what was going on within. None of us have a perfect life. We all go through something in some kind of way.

My wife and I have people who look at us and assume we are perfect. We fight very hard to dispel that idea, but we are convinced that people are going to believe what they want to believe regardless of what we say or do. My wife and I have spoken candidly about our desire to divorce weeks after we were married. We contemplated divorce at least once every other day for the first year of our marriage. It was rough. We did not see eye-to-eye on most things. She wanted her way and I wanted mine. I was not willing to compromise at all on most things. Plus, I was doing my best to lead with absolutely no training or experience. We went through premarital counseling and all that stuff. It was great for what it was, but I do not honestly believe it did much at all. We sat for hours and listened to all of these things on what we should and should not do. We laughed and cried together talking about how our marriage would look. Unfortunately, sitting in the premarital sessions was totally different than sitting in the bedroom together.

There were many nights were we went to bed angry with one another even though we knew we should not go to bed and still be angry with one another. We have thrown things at each other, said some really horrible things to each other, and really damaged one another emotionally. It is true that those closest to you can hurt you the most. This is because they know all the soft spots to stab the knife. Even though we argued and fought we continued to be a presence in the world by sharing our story of abstinence and purity in our courtship. We traveled the world sharing our belief in loving one another even while we were fighting. We would stand side-by-side with one another even though we were both upset. I am sure the image was beautiful and perfect, but our marriage was not—and is not—perfect.

Some years ago my wife asked me to sit down to dinner with this couple we recently met. They were quite the people and couple. Everything they did seemed excellent and over-the-top. They constantly tried to overshadow anything my wife and I said. They were overly affectionate to the point one would have to ask if what we were watching was real. Yes, you read that right. They would happily proclaim about being perfect and never having any real struggles of their own. The dinners and lunches were a bit too much for me to take in. I tried my best to get out of them as much as possible. But I had the Holy Spirit telling my wife and me to go dine with them.

There was this one dinner where I just became nauseated hearing all the things they were saying about their perfect life. I went to the bathroom, texted my wife, and asked her to meet me outside in five minutes. I was prepared to leave them at that table alone. After much talking and a VERY stern look, my wife convinced me to go back inside and finish our dinner date with the other couple. We walked back to the table and the other couple had the biggest smiles like someone took a happy stick and just smacked them with it. And please understand that I do not think happiness is not attainable in a marriage. I just knew something did not seem right between those two. It was almost a well-rehearsed skit unfolding at the dinner table. I also have a very low tolerance for anything that is not authentic. I am not a fan of small talk. I enjoy meaningful discussion where we are able to dive deep into our lives and really uncover things that were once hidden or buried. I like for conversation to have purpose and meaning. I want to be sharpened after talking. I do not like talking for the sake of talking. Nonetheless, they continued to put on their show.

After enduring yet another dramatic show of perfection from this couple, my wife and I were preparing to leave the restaurant. I opened my wife's car door, which allowed her to get in the car. She placed the key inside the ignition and started it up. While walking over to the driver's seat I heard my name being called. I turned to see the husband, of the couple I just mentioned, running in my direction. I will call him Tom. He ran over to me and asked if I was available for coffee or something so we could talk. You have been in a situation where your brain is screaming "NO!" but your mouth says "Sure!" Yes, I was in that situation. I tried my best to postpone the outing with him for as long as I could. Unfortunately, he was very adamant about talking. He made it seem like it was urgent—partly because he said it was.

We finally met up at a small diner in Jackson, Mississippi. He sat down with his cup of coffee and tears started to flow down his face. I would like to say I was stunned, but I would be lying. He bent his head low and said, "Brother, I am tired of living a lie." That was the first moment I felt anything real between us. He proceeded to tell me about the dysfunction in his home. His wife was domineering and very violent. He lost his job and he has been trying to cover it up by gambling throughout the day to match the amount of money he used to have coming in the house. He went on and on about all of the things happening in his life. My heart was deeply burdened listening to all of it. We sat and talked for hours. Then we prayed together.

He started listening to many of my sermons I have online. He was determined to not continue living a plastic life. I shared my struggles with him to the point he opened up more. I learned through that experience that people are more prone to open up when they know they are in an environment where trust and patience is plentiful. Tom and his wife did not have the best ending. Her violent tendencies drove him away. He later tried to find some kind of peace in alcohol and drugs. He and his wife eventually got divorced and went their separate ways. I have not heard from them since.

As stated mentioned earlier, we have all been in situations where we felt like we needed to paint a beautiful picture publicly while envying someone else's life privately. Do not take time to think about what you would do if you had someone else's life. Do not do that to yourself. Be thankful and grateful for what you have. You may not have as much as someone else, but you sure can make what you have just as great by being thankful for it.

Our society has become known for having more than what it really needs—myself included. We think having a lot means we are successful. That is not always true. I would rather have a few friends I could trust and really talk to instead of having many people around me for small talk and idle conversation. We much prefer quality over quantity.

There was a guy I knew who had multiple cars. I was jealous because of it. I had one car—a really great car. I look back now and understand my mistake. I was envious of the fact he had many cars when in actuality he could only drive one at a time. He could not take his fleet with him everywhere he went. I felt like having more was better. My car was just as great. I just needed to be thankful for it and be thankful I had a car when so many are without. Do you see the perspective we should have?

Do not spend your life being jealous or envious of other people—especially what you see on social media. It is all fluff anyway. We post our greatest moments and best images. If social media broadcasted the intimate parts of our life I am convinced many of us would be condemned straight to hell and proven false in many ways. Embrace and be thankful for the life you have. Be thankful for our Savior Jesus Christ and His sacrifice for our sins. He did not come to make bad men good; he came to make dead men live. He makes us truly alive with new life in Him. Our new life enables us to walk in freedom and truly explore the world in His eyes while preaching His message of grace, mercy, and love.

You must realize that you are not alone in how you are feeling. I would like to ask you to do a couple of things. First, I want you to write down on a separate piece of paper the names of those people you envy. Go ahead and write their names down. No one has to see the list. Be honest and thorough. Then, I want you to pray over that list. Call out their names one-by-one and pray for their wellbeing. Pray blessings and truth over their life. Pray that they abound and grow more in Christ. Pray for their safety and continued peace in their life. Continue praying for them daily. And ask God to change your heart towards them. Tell Him about your jealousy towards them. He already knows. You might as well confess it. You may ask why is it important to confess it if God already knows it. Well, confession means you are willing to be open and honest about the situation. It also means you are acknowledging the truth openly. Confession means you are bringing what was once hidden into the light voluntarily. It is a righteous thing. Do it and continue doing it.

Finally, I want you to always remember that you should not envy or be jealous of someone else's life. Do not think the grass is greener on the other side. In fact, noticing greener grass could be an indication you need to prune, fertilize, and tend to your own. I am amazed at how well we can tend to someone else's lawn while we allow ours to die. Envy and jealousy are grass killers. They are like weeds that suck the life out of your yard. Allow God to pluck those weeds up once-and-for-all. He is the Master Gardner. Let Him prune and cultivate.

You are not alone.

Chapter 7

FEAR OF FAILURE

Let me preface this chapter by saying I know our God has not given us the spirit of fear. He does not desire for us to live in worry or doubt. He fully expects us to trust Him and believe He will fulfill His promise(s) to us. However, I could not write this book without including my personal battle with the fear of failure. I have wrestled with the criticism I could face for being a preacher of hope who deals with the overwhelming fear of failure. But I must be honest, open, and transparent in hopes that someone reading these words will be convicted and encouraged by what they read. Here is my story.

The fear of failure cripples and incapacitates achievers. Successful people learn how to overcome their fear of failure and walk in victory. Overcoming the fear of failure is not as difficult as some may think. It has a lot to do with perspective. Unsuccessful people view their mistakes as personal, permanent, and immobilizing. Successful people view their mistakes as a reached outcome or finished result. They do not look at their mistakes as failures. They understand that their greatest successes can come from the trials and errors they experience. They grow content in learning from their mistakes because they know their mistakes do not mean they have completely failed.

Many people fail to act because they are afraid of possible failure. I know that was true for me for many years. I had to break out of that fear by taking appropriate action, staying faithful, and not taking things personally.

I believe I was bred to have a heavy desire for worldly success. Traveling and being exposed to more of the world outside of the small town I was born opened my eyes to opportunity and potential. I grew up around a family whose members were addicted to alcohol and drugs. They loved and cherished it. They even encouraged me to entertain myself with it at a young age. Seeing their lives stoked a passion inside of me to never be like them. I wanted something more out of life.

I was born in a very small town in Mississippi. Those I was around did not have much. I was raised with a greater emphasis on morals than things; respect rather than money. My mother—who was the primary leader and teacher in our home—was determined to teach and lead in such a way that my sister and I would aspire for more out of life. Seeing so much poverty and decay around me prompted a determination to gain more out of life than what I grew up seeing. I did not realize it at the time but a great determination comes with a very high price tag for failure. Any man who has ever set out to accomplish anything has had to deal with the idea that he will not accomplish his tasks and fulfill his dreams. That was my greatest struggle.

After hearing the Gospel preached and having my eyes opened to the truth, I became emboldened to live a life that is satisfactory to God. That means I had to lay down my own plans, dreams, and goals to allow God to instruct me on the way He desired for me to go. That in itself was a very difficult thing to do. Nevertheless, it had to be done. Every opportunity had to die; it had to cease from being an option in my life. The only way it could live was if God gave it life. I could no longer be the originator. I had to follow His way; lead by His example; go in His truth. I wanted to follow my own way and chart my own course. I was your typical overachiever. I graduated high school with more credits than I needed and a dual degree. I was an active member of more than seventeen different organizations in high school like the Future Business Leaders of America, Future Farmers of America, Beta Club, National Honor Society, etc. And I had the opportunity to serve as a leading officer in many of them. I also founded a mentoring organization while in high school called Gentlemen of Quality or GQ. I had both a zero and seventh period—two separate classes that were not mandatory for me to take. I had ambition to excel and be the very best at everything. My problem was my hope was in my own ability. My tenacity and ambition to excel was motivated by one thing—a gnawing fear of failure.

My fear of failure caused me to concentrate on what others thought about me. I was never a popular kid growing up. I did not have the best of things—which are oftentimes used as the evidence for popularity in life. I did not garner any type of attention from anyone except the attention I gained from being overweight. It seemed like people would always point out my weight problem, and that brought me great shame. The constant jeers and comments made about my appearance were many. Everyone had a joke about the way I looked. Have you ever had people watch you while you eat and laugh? Well, I have, and I can tell you that it is not fun. I hated the way I looked, and there were many times I cried out wishing I were dead.

Shame is a toxic emotion seeing that it makes one feel bad about who he is as a person instead of feeling bad about his actions. And a man is dangerous if he has no remorse for his hate-driven actions. His ability to focus on feeling bad for himself causes him to almost blot out and/or justify his actions—whether good or bad—because how of he feels about himself. My shame brought light to my fear of failure. The desire of not wanting to be exposed and made fun of caused me to retreat inwardly and build a wall around me in the hopes others would accept me even though I did not accept myself. My shame also caused me to make excuses for my inability to act appropriately in certain situations. It also caused me to do whatever I thought I needed to do to win.

You must remember that shame brings more awareness to your ego than your actions. It focuses all the attention on self while ignoring the actions. Since I focused so much on self it became easy for me to manipulate and swindle others to achieve whatever I set my mind to do. I was becoming a very wicked man. Shame separates the man from the crowd because he does not want to be looked upon as being different, he then becomes an island to himself. His loneliness breeds depression and anger. That was definitely true for me. I was angry at the world, and I felt like everyone in it needed to pay for the way I was treated in my life.

The fear of failure also made me think no one would like to befriend me. So I did my best to keep to myself. I put up a very high wall of armor around my heart. I became afraid of anyone loving me mainly because I felt like her love was not genuine, she could not truly love me, and I was not capable of being loved. I was embarrassed and put to shame about my image and I felt everyone around me would feel the same way about it. This made my marriage very difficult in the beginning. I fought against any love my wife tried to show me. I would cringe any time she told me she loved me and became angry when she said we would be together forever. I felt like she was living in a fairy tale world. I did not understand how anyone could love someone like me seeing that I did not truly love myself. My wife and I had many arguments because of it. This handicap kept me from many beneficial friendships. I refused to allow anyone to get too close me. I would find a reason to end the friendship if I felt like the person was getting to close to me.

Unlike others who may have a fear of failure I did not lower my expectations. I know some who have shared with me their nagging fear of failure. It caused them to lower their expectations of themselves so they would not disappoint themselves or others. They did not want to have a diminished opinion of those they valued. This caused them to do little to nothing. The very idea of moving forward was oftentimes halted by the idea they would fail in whatever they tried to do and others would be disappointed in them. It is like failing in a race you have yet to enter. And no man can win unless he firsts begin.

I look back over my life and remember many things I failed to win at simply because I was too afraid to even try. The fear of failing at something I was not comfortable doing caused me to shrink back in more fear and remain stagnant. I failed at 100% of the things I didn't even attempt. I failed completely.

My fear of failure really began to show after I was illuminated to the knowledge and lordship of Jesus. I was inundated with rules and laws that I knew I could not obey. This caused me to rebel. I understood that breaking a single piece of the law means I broke the entire thing. That was a tough pill for me to swallow. Since I could not completely follow all the laws I was given, either over the pulpit or based on the Levitical rules, I chose to live recklessly. My fear of failing a piece of the law kept me from attempting to uphold some of it—at least. It took me learning about the beautiful sacrifice of Christ to understand how wrong I was.

Jesus' sacrifice fulfilled the law in its entirety. Therefore, I would no longer be subject to the law; instead, I am subject to Him. He is the completion; He is the fulfillment. It does not end there. Before Jesus ascended to His heavenly throne He told the disciples not to be sorrowful because He was sending the Helper, who is the Holy Spirit. He stands in Jesus' place on earth. Having the Holy Spirit is like walking daily with Jesus. He is not an ominous figure floating around like a ghost; He is the third Person of the Trinity, which is the Father, the Son, and the Holy Spirit. He provides a beautiful conviction that pierces the soul and pleads the case for holiness. He leads us in a way that we will not cause us to fall into temptation. He guides so we will not slip back into our old way of living. He takes over and continues the work started by our Savior, Jesus Christ.

The indwelling power of the Holy Spirit completely eradicates fear and saturates the vessel He resides with faith. He is the reason I realized I no longer have to fear. Why would I fear anything if He is with me? He guides me. He convicts me. He comforts me. Many who say they are within the Body of Christ have started to dismiss the presence of the Holy Spirit. That is blasphemy—complete blasphemy! Many who dismiss Him do so because they do not know Him. If one truly believes in the saving power of Christ and has confessed Him as Lord then he should also believe in the One Jesus sent to stand in His place. The initial man, Adam, was told by God in Genesis that it is not good for man to be alone. Jesus, who was there at man's formation, realized it was not good to leave man alone either. So He gave us the Holy Spirit to help just like God gave Eve to Adam to help. Do not ignore the beautiful and powerful presence of the Holy Spirit. Confess Jesus as Lord and Savior. Pray, which is our communication with God, for Him to give you the Holy Spirit to abide in you, guide you, and convict you. He will do it! I am sure of it.

It is my hope and prayer that you understand the magnitude of how much you are missing in your life because of your fear of failure. I personally know men who do nothing because they feel like they will fail at everything. Their inability to be obedient places a heavier burden on those who are faithful in obedience. I pity no man who sits idly by while work needs to get done. The fear of failure always places the blame on someone else. The response of the fearful is, "I will just wait for someone else to do it." I know that way of living because I have lived it before. However, I cannot afford to live that way right now. I must act. I had a major revelation one day that really helped me to understand the danger of my fear of failure and how it was like poison to my life. I want to share it with you before closing.

The foundation of the fear of failure is failure. The very idea of failing seems more than what most can handle. We have grown accustomed to the notion that failure is always a bad thing. That is not entirely correct. Some of my greatest lessons have come because of failure. It was in those moments that I learned what I should and should not do the next time. I was running from the idea that failure would ruin me when I was already ruined because I failed to try. I look back over my life and cringe at all the things I could have done, all the places I should have visited, all the things I should have said, but did not because of fear. It paralyzes you from action and it stunts our growth. Every opportunity I am given is one I seek to capitalize and learn from.

Some may look at the outcome and say I failed while I believe I learned something I did not know before. I simply refuse to sit around on the sidelines while everyone is facing their fears in the game. I have had countless people tell me what I could and could not do. I was told I could never publish a book. I did. Some said my wife and I would never stay married after a year. We are. Others said we could not start a church in Atlanta. We have. Has every step been easy? Absolutely not! However, each opportunity teaches me something new. It keeps me on my knees in prayer.

So, do not think you are alone in your fear of failure. I feared failing my wife, and, honestly, I have failed her many times. I have not been the perfect husband. I feared failing my son. Honestly, I have not been the perfect father. I have failed him many times. I feared failing my church as a pastor. And I have failed them many times. But I know my God's grace is sufficient and His mercies are new every morning. Each failure has been a new opportunity to learn and mature. We are all failures in some way or another. The important thing is to realize that having failed does not make you a failure and it should never define who you are. In fact, the only action to take after one has failed is to overcome.

Some may want to classify themselves as failures. Well, they can do that. As for me and my house, we are overcomers. We do not settle for mediocrity; we excel far beyond the status quo. We get up every time we have fallen down. We are not just conquerors; we are more than conquerors! It is time to act. What is something you have been told by our God to do but have not done it because of your fear of failure? I want you to do something very bold. Go ahead and do it as He leads you. Will it be uncomfortable? Yes! Will it cost you more than what you have right now? Absolutely! Will it mean you will have to mature above who you are right now? Of course! But do not hesitate to act. It gets easier and easier and easier with each step you take. You are not alone! It is time to walk by faith. Because it is faith, you will not see the physical manifestation of your work immediately. Just continue believing. I also encourage you to read a copy of a book I wrote, *Learning How to Walk: Inspiring Others to Walk by Faith.* It will strengthen and encourage your walk of faith and prompt you to step out of fear.

Chapter 8

CHASING "NORMAL"

Growing up a short, fat kid had its advantages and disadvantages. I was always offered food, which was a great thing because I loved to eat. Honestly, I felt like that was my only advantage. I felt like my disadvantages were many. I was constantly ridiculed and mocked because of my weight. I did not get attention from girls like the other boys. I was not athletically inclined. I just did not feel like one of the guys. I felt like I was an outcast—an island all to myself. My insecurities were many, and they were deep. I was oftentimes ridiculed for my "man breasts"—the swelling of breast tissue that is caused by an imbalance of estrogen and testosterone (most men don't even realize they have breast tissue).

I always felt uncomfortable no matter what I wore. I felt like people were looking at my chest. This was one of the major issues I had to deal with. They hung low, and I was the subject of many jokes because of them. I actually received a bra as a "gift" during my freshman year of high school. I tried to laugh it off as if it were funny, but the laughing did nothing to curb the pain and embarrassment I felt. The laughs grew louder as people came up to me to view my chest and examine it to see if the bra was big enough. That was very traumatic for me. It was an issue I did not want to cope with because it was very embarrassing. Enlarged male breasts can be reduced for some men, but that was not the case for me. I felt like they were continuing to grow daily. Was I self-conscious about them? Absolutely! I tried to convince my doctor to cut them off. When he resisted and told me to allow my body to naturally balance itself I tried to take matters into my own hands. I grabbed a knife, went into our bathroom, and attempted to cut them off myself. Was I successful? Thankfully not. I barely made a scratch before I realized how stupid of a mistake I was making. All I knew is that I was chasing after the idea of being "normal." At that time, I defined being normal as having a flat chest, a six-pack of abs, and smooth talking skills to speak to the ladies. I wanted to be one of the guys. I wanted to fit in, and I was willing to do whatever I had to do to attain it.

I struggled with a large chest all of my childhood and a great deal of my young adult life. I tried everything from compression shirts to homemade straps to tighten it down and give the impression of a flat chest. My homemade straps were simply an old piece of shirt I cut up that I wrapped around my chest very tightly. I would tie a knot in it so it would not fall off during the day. It had no real support so there were times when I would be walking and it would fall to the ground. I have also been embarrassed when people would touch my back and feel the homemade strap. I would get asked whether or not I was wearing a bra. It was very embarrassing. I tried diet pills and green tea that was supposed to decrease breast tissue. Nothing seemed to work. The chase of being "normal" was so intense that I did not care how I attained it. Many people told me my body would straighten out as I got older, but I did not want to wait for it. I felt like God hated me. I did not understand why He would allow me to develop the enlarged breast tissue and be subject countless jokes. Experiencing it made me question His entire existence. I know this may sound crazy to you. One would question why I would doubt God's existence just because my body was different. However, that was my reality. Was it right? No. Do I feel that way now? I do not. It was definitely something I had to overcome.

My freshman year of high school was extremely tough. I grew up in the country, backwoods of Mississippi. I was in school with mostly Caucasians. In 2000, my family moved to Riverdale, Georgia. The high school was mostly African-American, and the hip-hop culture ruled the halls and classroom conversations. I knew nothing about it. It was definitely difficult for me. I grew up listening to foot-stomping, knee-slapping church music from artists like Shirley Caesar and the Mighty Clouds of Joy and some of the raunchiest Blues singers you will ever hear like Tyrone Davis and Shirley Brown. Those two distinct genres of music ruled my house and all the homes I entered while growing up. The closest I got to hip-hop was one song by Coolio, "Gangster's Paradise." I had absolutely no clue what the song was about, but I knew the words.

Moving from a place of church music and Blues to a culture dominated by hip-hop was very difficult for me. I struggled with the change in scenery, the change of people, the change in conversation, and my overweight frame. A group of senior boys saw fit to constantly chastise me. They would steal my food while I was eating lunch and make me chase them around the cafeteria while everyone erupted in laughter. I was the butt of the jokes partly because my butt was larger than everyone else's. I cannot count how many times I wanted to kill myself. I hated the way I looked. I hated taking pictures. I hated looking in the mirror. I just hated myself.

Before courting my wife in 2009, I had not taken a picture since my senior photos in 2004. I did not want to take the senior photos, but I felt it was the right thing to do at the time. I told my mom I would do it so she would have an updated picture to remember me by and put in my obituary in case something happened to me. That was my main reason. I bought the smallest package of pictures and I did not give any of them out. I threw most of them away. My hatred for my body and myself was deep—very deep. That deep insecurity has followed until this point of my life. I still battle with it. On top of all of that, the pain was also deep.

I did not know the Lord at that time. I constantly compared myself to other guys, and I always felt as if I came up short. I still compare myself to other men. I always envied the guys who walked around freely without a shirt on. It was just the little things for me that I felt many guys took for granted. I envied the guys who were comfortable with jumping in the pool without a shirt on. My insecurity with my body helped me to stay out of water. I was the boy at the pool with two shirts on as if everyone could not see my chest imprint. The summers were brutal because I still wore more clothes than required so I could hide my body. I remember sweating profusely under my shirt, but it did not matter. I would just put another shirt on top of it. There were days I would be wearing an excess of four different shirts. They made me look much larger than I was. I did not care though. I was embarrassed. It was something I did not talk about with others. I just did not want them to know my pain and shame even though many of them could see it by the way I tried to hide it. I tried my best to appear as normal as possible, but that did not always work. It was just awkward.

During the winter months of my freshman year of high school my mom bought me a large, puffy bubble jacket. It truly served its purpose during the winter months, but it served a greater purpose for me--it helped to hide my enlarged chest. I wore the jacket everyday. It was my little piece of security. It was my hiding place so others would not have to look at my body. It served as my fig leaf to hide my shame. It looked appropriate to wear in the winter months, but it became an unneeded piece of apparel when it started to get warm outside. I did not really need it in the first place. I actually enjoy the cold weather. I wore it because it served as an extra piece of clothing to hide what I hated and cover up what I knew I could not get rid of. Ouch! That actually hurt to write. Can you empathize with me on that?

I met a husband and wife who did all they could to hide their special needs child from the world. They rarely came out in public because they did not want their child seen. They were doing the same thing I was doing—trying to hide what they hated and cover up what they knew they could not get rid of. They were also in pursuit of the idea of having a "normal" child.

I have met women who were addicted to makeup. They are completely different people after their makeup is applied. It gives them confidence and security. They, too, try to hide what they hate and cover up what they know they cannot get rid of. My bubble coat was my security blanket. What is yours? What do you hide behind? What are you trying to cover up? Is it a job title?

It is an article of clothing? Is it designer clothes? What is it for you? It may be difficult to admit, but it is time for you to come clean about it. It is time to admit it. It is important that you admit it. It is also important to identify what you believe is "normal." In doing so you will open your eyes to a truth you may not have known existed.

I wrote earlier about what I thought was normal. I also wrote about how I was trying to fit in with the other guys. I even played football—even though I hate sports—just so I could feel somewhat normal. I was chasing after an image that was not real or attainable mainly because it was a figment of my imagination. I formed my idea of what was normal from what I saw on television and the people around me. I saw all the other guys with flat chests and smaller frames. I wanted that look. It did not occur to me that even their frames were different. I was trying to chase after this perfect image while ignoring the perfection of how I was created. I was so dissatisfied with myself that I never looked in the mirror to accept who God created me to be.

I am much smaller than I was back then, but the insecurity still exists. I cannot stand on a stage without thinking whether the crowd is looking at me or questioning whether or not I am overweight. I do not deal with the enlarged breast issue any longer; however, it still haunts me. Although they are not there, I still live with the residual memory as if they do. I have logged many hours of hard work in the gym chasing after this idol of a perfect body image. I have reached my goals before only to be dissatisfied with my body all over again. I remember going from almost 220 pounds to 155 pounds. One would think I would be happy, right? Wrong. I still found something wrong with me. I began to hate the way my feet looked. Then I hated the color of my eyes. I was never satisfied. I could only imagine how God feels knowing I hate what I believe He created. Have you experienced that before? Have you ever reached a goal only to create a new one because you were not satisfied?

I have had to ask myself this question many times in my life: What is normal? This world feeds us so many lies about what they believe normal is and what it is not. We live in a world of Photoshop and digital imagining. We are able to manipulate a picture any way we would like to make it look the way we want. I have read stories about little girls who regurgitate their food so they can maintain an ideal bodyweight or little boys who join gangs in search of the comfort of a family. We come into this world searching for something to attach onto. Like newborn babies, we are looking to suck on the breast of the world. Sadly enough, many do not get weaned off of it. This is why it is so important to taste and see the goodness of the Lord. One taste of Jesus will completely erase your taste for sin. That is a truth that cannot be ignored. We live in a world that is trying to run away from anything that is different. That is ironic, seeing that we are all different in some way or another. We run away from the idea of being different even though we are essentially all different. No two people are exactly alike. Comparing ourselves to one another serves no good purpose. In fact, comparing belittles; it does not edify. Comparing myself to other men does not edify the gifts and image God gave me. It makes me ungrateful for my gifts and image and covet what does not belong to me. It also denies us the opportunity to experience and receive from the gift of others. We are all unique. We must develop a willingness to accept our differences and become content in who we are as individuals.

I have stood in my closet before and had the nerve to say I did not have anything to wear. That was such a lie. I had something to wear. The problem was I did not want to wear it. I felt like my clothes were outdated because I had worn them before. How terrible! Traveling over to Ethiopia allowed me to see how ungrateful I am. Some of the men I met only had two shirts and a pair of pants. They washed their clothes in a creek by their home that was made out of tin and straw. Even though they had little, they acted as though it was worth everything. They took very good care of it.

I have lived with the idea that having more means I am doing better. That is not always true. In fact, there are some cases where having less is better than having more. I remember the days when I did not have a cell phone. My friends would have to call me on our house phone. That was always an interesting experience especially when my parents answered the phone. Nevertheless, technology was not as advanced as it is now. We did not have the social media phenomenon we have now. The only way we could catch up with each other was through a very slow dial-up connection that featured a minimally functional email account and chat rooms filled with mostly perverts and pedophiles.

When texting emerged in my world it was too cumbersome to even try. My son is definitely growing up in a different world than I did. Getting in contact with someone to a more personal aspect back then. It was less technological, but it was also less intrusive and less demanding. Those days were a little calmer because there were less ways to reach out to people.

They were a little more personal. Those were the days where less was definitely better.

It is normal in our day to have great technological advances. We can reach people around the world in the matter of seconds. Our technology advances daily, and it is advancing at a rapid speed. The "normal" we have today may not be the normal we have tomorrow. The concept of social media and being closer to someone around the globe than your next-door neighbor is normal in our day. That concept is still progressing and it will continue to progress until there is a new normal. Why is this important? It is important because we are forever chasing the idea of what it is to be normal. Ecclesiastes, one of the many Books of the Bible, describes this chase as chasing after the wind. It references it as foolish. Have you ever tried to get a hold of a cloud? It cannot be done. There is nothing there to hold. Trying to grab the wind is futile and pointless, and yet that is what many of us are trying to do. The chase is just not worth the time we invest in it. Honestly, many of us are addicted to the idea of "new." Many are quick to run to purchase the newest phones, clothing, or other expensive gadgets. Many want to feel as if they have the newest thing and are involved in the newest trend because many believe "new" is always better.

What are you chasing? What are you running after? You must know that lust and envy, which are the foundation of the chase, are never satisfied. The eyes always want to see more. The ears are not satisfied with what they hear. They desire something more. Many spend more time chasing money, an overly demanding career, philosophy, friendships, marriage, popularity, sensations (drugs, sex, etc.), the latest diet fads, the latest fashion trends, the list is endless. Many are dissatisfied with their life because they fail to realize their pursuit of worldly enjoyment and fulfillment is a lie. Nothing in this world will fulfill you.

I had the opportunity of meeting a father and husband who worked hard to climb the corporate ladder and reach the second highest office in the company. He started as an entry-level employee. It was an encouraging story, but it came with a heavy price. His climbing through the ranks of the company meant he had to give more of his time and energy to the company. He was no longer available for his son's football games. He was not home in time to help his children with their homework. He did not get a chance to sit with them at the table at night to discuss their day. His wife longed and missed his presence because he was rarely at home. As he continued to climb the ranks, he had to work on Saturdays and Sundays—on occasion. He was missing many of the crucial moments of his children's lives. He tried to make it up to them by buying them whatever they wanted. He took them on their yearly vacation but spent most of his time on his phone discussing business. His excuse was always the same—this is my job; I have to work. He felt like doing for them was enough.

I came to know about his story because of his son, who was about my age. He told me his story after he came to me for help. He was hungry for a man's affection. He thirsted for attention and affirmation from his father, but his father proved he was not available for him. His father proved that he did not have the time to devote to investing in him by choosing him over work. His father tried to paint the picture that he was trying to provide a better life for his family. In actuality, he was ruining his family by not providing the most important thing they needed—him.

They did not need the expensive toys or vacations. They needed, and wanted, him. They hungered for his presence. The young man hungered so much for his presence that he started to look for it in strip clubs. When the strip clubs stopped fulfilling him he started going to local bathhouses to have sex with complete strangers—both men and women. His appetite for affection and attention became voracious and extremely dangerous. He did not realize that he, too, was chasing after something that would never fulfill him. He wanted love but all he was finding was lust. He and his dad were chasing worldly things to fill their God-sized hole. After a much-needed conversation and praying together, they ended their pursuit of the world and surrendered themselves to Jesus. They gave up the worldly chase.

What are you chasing? I had a young man tell me one time that he did not have time to pray. I quickly had to correct him. He had time to pray. His problem was not time; his problem was desire. He had no desire to pray. His heart was filled with the stress and cares of the world. It desired and hungered what he felt the world could give him. I asked him to come sit in my office and bring his calendar. He looked at me and said, "Why do you want to see my calendar?" It was simple. A man's schedule shows you a great deal about him. It shows where he places his most valuable asset—his time.

You cannot place the pursuit of things over quiet time with the Lord. You cannot prize time with friends and extracurricular activities more than you prize time with your families. It is time to expose our worthless pursuit for what it is— idolatry. It is an empty pursuit for earthly comfort. It is time to stop the empty chase.

Many are looking to find their identity in what they "do." I will use myself for example. I preach. Being called a "preacher" does not define who I am. I am a Christ follower. I preach because of who I am. Christ gives me identity. Then I get my activity based on my identity. I get purpose out of my identity, not the other way around. The world says, "Find your purpose then get your identity." Jesus says, " Abide in me." We then get our purpose after we find identity in Him. I have met young adults who are pursing careers because of the pressure placed on them by their parents or counselors. They claim to be followers of Christ yet they are chasing the world. Their pursuit is empty and worthless.

A job title will not fulfill you. I thought it would fulfill me. I aspired to have an office with a name placard on the desk. I wanted a great job title that required me to wear suits and order people to do things. I finally realized that desire. I got the office, the mandate to wear suits, the name placard on my desk, everything. I thought it would fulfill my desires and make me feel special. After obtaining it, I felt like a slave in a suit. I was chasing after a dream that meant absolutely nothing. I am thankful I did not have children or a wife at the time. I worked 14 to 16 hours a day at times. It was very intense. I still did not feel any better once I laid my head down to sleep at night. It was truly like I was trying to catch the wind in a fish net.

What are you chasing? If it is not God then it does not matter. Stop the empty pursuit.

Chapter 9

BEHIND CLOSED DOORS

I have often wondered what I would find if I peeked behind closed doors. What would I uncover in the deep shadows of darkness and night where we think we hide our best sin? I do not have to look far; I can simply peek behind my own door.

I have suffered a lot due to the wrong and danger of my ways. Could I ever be truly set free from the bondage of my past and the pain of my present circumstances? I would think so. Well, I know I can. My heart longs to be so selfless that I begin to see others the way God sees them—to see them through eyes of love and mercy. I desire to peer behind their closed doors and encourage them to come from behind them and embrace a culture of freedom and grace that is found only in Jesus Christ. We know the Father loved; therefore, He sent the Son, who is Jesus, to save the world, not judge it. For the world was already judged. How so? Well, the Light has come; however, men love darkness more than they love the Light because their deeds are evil. They, or I should say we, love the darkness and choose to hide behind closed doors so we are not exposed. We do not want the messiest parts of our life all in the streets. We could not live with knowing that others are aware of our deepest desires and our sinful thoughts. Therefore, we live behind closed doors.

I do not want you to imagine natural doors; I want you to think of the doors that open to your soul. I want to dive deep in the area of your heart that has not been penetrated since the hurt or the pain you encountered. That is where I intend on taking you thorough this chapter. It may seem like surgery to you. Take my explanation of what I am about to do as our pre-surgery appointment. I want you to prepare you heart and mind for this journey we are about to take as we burst open the doors you have tried to keep closed for so long. It is time for you to walk out and realize that you are not alone.

Darkness shields itself from the light. It shelters itself so it will not cease from existing, which is its fate if it is confronted with light. I felt invincible and invisible while hiding away in the darkness. It was there that I was able to truly be myself, enjoy my perverted thoughts, and feast on the worldly affections without the threat of ridicule. It was my personal oasis of freedom—or so I thought. I was under the illusion of freedom even though I was trapped inside a cell of sin. Why was it an illusion? Well, the darkness causes the eyes not to see as well as they would in light. I could not see the bars; I did not know they were there. I was able to sit in that cell and dine on my lustful ways all while wishing I was noticed and amongst people who would accept me for my past, my present, and my future.

Being alone in the darkness was tiring and terribly dreadful! It was in the darkness that I hid all of my insecurities. I drug all the fat jokes, inappropriate touches, bitterness, and jealousy into that cell with me. There I sat alone for a great majority of my life because I did not want to face the light and truly be exposed because, honestly, I was afraid! I was afraid of what others would say about me. I was afraid of what others would do to me. I was afraid of my past coming back to haunt me. I had no more tears to cry or words to say. All I could do was sit in that cell in utter darkness and groan from time to time.

I only wonder what kind of cell you find yourself in right now. Are you ashamed of the molestation, hurt by the indifference towards it, and angry because you cannot stop reliving it over and over again in your head? Are you ashamed of the lustful thoughts you have for the same-sex? Are you really hiding away in the shadows of darkness so others will not know the thoughts of your mind? Are you hiding because of the way you look? Is it your weight, your teeth, your hair, your eyes, your nose, or your entire body that causes you to hide away in the darkness? What is it? Are you like some who try to hide behind sports, food, sex, or some other diversion to fill the empty void of your soul? What is your medication? Is it pornography? Honestly, that was my go-to medicine to soothe my perverse appetite. The pictures and people in the movies never took time to judge me. I did not have to hold a conversation with them. I did not have worry about them gossiping about me. I did not have to introduce them to my family. I could enjoy their presence and actions without having to connect with them personally. It is the height and depth of selfishness, but I did not care. I wanted what I wanted, and there was no one in the darkness to stop me or tell me I was wrong. I have known some to turn to drugs, alcohol, food, and the like to fill their God-sized holes in their soul. Their gluttonous appetite was not satisfied by anything other than the pleasure this world has to offer no matter how filthy or nasty it could be.

I oftentimes wondered what separated me from those who openly lived their perverted lives in the light for others to see. There was a time in my life where I envied them. I desperately wanted to be them. I saw their lives as being true and really free. That is beginning of the "come-out-of-the-closet" mentality. I had to work my way up to one key thing that would cause me to join their cause and flaunt my sin in the streets for all to see. I needed to quench any truth within me until I grew cold against anything that resembled the Holy God. There was no way I could serve two masters; I would have to love one and hate the other. In short, I would have to hate God and turn from Him completely. I had to grow numb to Him, and the darkness was becoming a safe place to do it.

My knowledge of the truth quickly began to grow as my eyes opened more to the truth. I began to see the bars that kept me locked inside for so many years. Then, I heard the Gospel message about Jesus setting me free from the bondage of sin and the consequences of hell. The bars, although large and thick, did not seem to scare me any longer. In fact, hearing the Gospel message was like sweet music to my ears and it brought freedom to my heart and soul. I do not know about you, but I got excited after hearing it preached. I knew freedom was ahead. There was only one problem—I was stuck in that cell of sin. As I sat there I began to hear a freeing sound. It was the rattling of keys. That may not mean much to you, but it meant freedom to me.

I'll give you an example so you get a better grasp of what I am writing here. Two men sleep in their cell at the state corrections center. They have been in that cell for almost twenty-two hours straight. One could imagine the two of them are growing testy and contentious. They are like wild lions ready to tear one another limb from limb. While they sleep to pass the time away they hear the sound of keys rattling. They both jump up from their sleep in excitement and rush over to the steel door that locks them out of true freedom. The sound of the keys is getting closer and closer to their cell door. They are anticipating the moment they are able to walk out of the cell. The guard comes closer and closer and closer with the keys. He stands in front of the cell with the keys in his hand. He inserts the key in the lock and turns it until it pops open. The doors finally swing open and the men—who were once imprisoned—are set free. Those men were excited to hear the rattling of the keys because that was their way to escape the drudgery and torment of the cell. That was my reaction after hearing the Gospel.

The issue still remained—the Light had come to open the door of the cell, but I was a lover of darkness. I feared stepping out of the cell because I did not want to be exposed. I knew the Light would expose me. Years ago, I watched a television show where an old man had spent more than seventeen years in prison. He had a long list of offences, and he had been in and out of the jail system for most of his life. He went before the parole board to state his claim of why he should be released from prison. I was surprised by his response. He told them it would be best if they kept him locked up in the cell because that is all he knew. He told them he would rather stay in prison than go out into the freedom of the world. He had never worked a real job in his life. He never had a place of his own. He did not have a driver's license. He did not know how to work a smartphone. He was ignorant of so much, but he was not ignorant to the fact that he knew he would be exposed for what he did not know if he truly stepped out into the light of the world. He would feel ashamed and embarrassed if he tried to get a job and they found out he did not know how to really go about it. His writing and reading skills were at an elementary level. He was socially awkward. He knew all this, and he did not want to be exposed for it. So, what did he do? He chose to request to stay in the darkness. You may read that and think he is such a fool for wanting to skip out on true freedom just so he can stay in bondage. I ask that you turn the mirror to yourself and righteously judge your own life. Do you run from the light in fear that you will be exposed? Are you still practicing secret sin? If so, you are no different than the prisoner who chose to request to stay locked behind bars. When given the chance to walk out of the cell, he declined just like you.

There is a beautiful thing I love about leaving the cell. It is truly embracing the light. Light does expose what is going on in the darkness. It is not something that should be ignored; instead, it should be embraced. We should desire the light and the judgment it brings. Did I just write that? Oh my! Yes, I wrote it, and I meant it. We should be eternally thankful for the righteous judgment it brings. A man walks into his house and hears grunts and groans coming from upstairs. He grabs a bat from his garage and races upstairs to figure it out if everything and everyone in his house is okay. He checks the children's rooms to find they are not home. He still hears the grunts and groans coming from the last room down the hallway—which is the room he shares with his wife. He bursts into the dark room, and the first thing he does is turns on the light. The noise stops, and because of the light, he can see that his wife is in the bed with

BEHIND CLOSED DOORS

another man. It is at that moment the affair has come to light, and it was being judged righteously. It was wrong from the start, but the darkness hid it away from being seen. Once the husband saw it he was able to judge it—righteously.

The adulterer quickly jumped from the bed exposing his naked body to the wife's husband. He quickly grabbed his things while trying to avoid the swings of the husband's baseball bat. The wife sits upright in the bed with tears flowing down her eyes. She has been caught! The light has been turned on! Her darkness is no more! She has been exposed! Many will look at that and think that it is a bad thing for her. In actuality, it is the best thing that could have happened to her. Her humiliation and exposure could bring about repentance and change. It could stop her from making those types of decisions in the future, cause her to rethink her actions, and seriously think about the hurt she caused her family and friends. She brought shame to her house, but the exposure from the light brought about serious judgment. And judgment can bring about repentance.

I encourage you to run towards the light. Practically, that means you confess your sins. Confession is an act of true freedom. I have felt such freedom many times in my short life. I have also felt the bondage of lying—the nemesis of confession. I remember my mother coming home to find a kitchen full of dishes. She was irate. She came in the living room where I was sitting and asked me, "Son, did you leave those dishes in the sink?" With a nervous disposition, I replied, "No, ma'am." I lied, and I was willing to hide away in the darkness. I knew I created the big mess in the kitchen, but I did not want to truly admit it and be exposed for my actions. My mom went around the house

101

and asked my sister and father the same question. Not surprisingly, they had the answer as I did. My mom was furious all over again. While she was in the kitchen she noticed my watch on the counter. She knew I always took it off when I cooked. The evidence was there; all I needed to do was confess. She asked me again with a very stern look and seriousness in her voice. I broke down and confessed my actions. I was definitely disciplined for my actions. What stuck out to me the most was my mom's response to me. She said, "Son, I can deal with a dirty kitchen, but I cannot deal with a lying child!" It would seem that my lying overrode the fact I left a dirty kitchen. She was more upset that I refused to confess my actions than she was about the dishes in the sink. I also realized that I could have quickly resolved the entire issue if I had just confessed in the beginning. However, I did not. I allowed for this entire event to continue—causing friction and anger in our home. I learned a valuable lesson that day, and I pray you have learned from my shame. Go ahead and confess your sins. I was weighted down for most of my life because of the things I carried within. I had to let them go, and confession was my method. I had to confess my anger against my father's silence, the perversion of my heart, my manipulative ways, and so on. I remember screaming out in the woods at God to tell Him how difficult it felt to forgive those who abused and misused me. My confession turned to tears. But they were not tears of sorrow; they were tears of joy. I felt like the cage door was being released. I was finally set free from the bondage of my past. I was able to live in the light and no longer ashamed of my past.

Please understand that I would not ask you to do anything

I would not do. This book is filled with confession. I have laid it all out for you. I ask that you do the same thing. James writes that we should confess out faults one to another and pray for one another (James 5:16). I encourage you to do just that. Confess your sins. Come in to the Light and know the Son, who is Jesus Christ, sets you free.

Chapter 10

STRUGGLING IN SILENCE

Many in certain religious denominations are adamant about calling those things that be not as though they were. For them it is an act of working their faith and pretending to be mini-gods. They use their words to create their desired future. It is essentially a repackaging of New Age beliefs in Christian jargon. Nevertheless, their desire to speak the future into existence limits them from actually recognizing and dealing with the present. They get so caught up in calling the things that be not as though they were that they fail to actually confront the things that are and intentionally deal with them.

The pain in your heart is there. Out of it flows so many other issues and struggles. Constantly pushing it away does nothing to help. I know it does not because I did it for years. I purposely would not talk about the issues of my heart. I would suppress them. I did not want to talk about the anger I felt from having a present yet absent father. I did not want to talk about the insecurity birthed from feeling inadequate as a youth. I did not want to deal with my pornography addiction that had driven me to build a mountain of lust in my heart. I soon began to desire anyone who desired me.

I spent many years of my life trying to find my sexual

identity. Curiosity and lust is a dangerous mix. I know because I was drinking that cocktail daily, and it was stirring a lustful and perverse desire in me. I felt like I was being baited to choose a sexual preference based on attraction, not truth. The cocktail of lust I constantly drank had me double-minded. I was not sure who I liked, and my attraction to some was not considered normal. I was intoxicated by lust; therefore, I was not thinking soberly. Instead, I constantly fed the lust brewing in my heart and continued to indulge my lustful desires. It was a struggle that would follow me into my teenage and adult years. It was not a desire I sought after or one I believe I was born with. I did not emerge from my mother's womb craving the sexual fulfillment from anyone who would have me. I believe it was something that continued to build in me as I continued to watch pornography and engage in sensual conversation. I tried and desired to engross myself in every fantasy I could imagine.

I dove into a world of imagination and sexual fulfillment. It was a quiet and private world. It was one I wanted to hide from everyone. I did not want others to explore it with me. I wanted to walk that lonely road alone. It was also a world I did not want to be in but one I chose to be in because of my lustful choices. I was drowning in an ocean of perversion. I became desensitized to what I knew was right—which was a pure attraction to my one-day wife. Soon enough I lowered all restraints and tried to fulfill every fantasy I watched. The constant entertainment began to bore me; I wanted action, and I was willing to compromise everything to get it.

Pornography was my opening—my portal to lustful adventure. I was already very insecure about my body.

Pornography allowed me to fulfill sexual encounters and fantasy without having to show myself. It did not require me to meet parents, go on dates, have in depth conversation, or purchase gifts on major holidays. I saw my requirement as minimal. In fact, I was giving up more than I would ever have given in a righteous relationship. I was giving my entire life and soul to a perverse and dark world that was eating me from the inside out. Sadly, I felt like I was all alone and no one would understand me. As I got older I began to see that pornography, although dangerous, was the main way I would seek satisfaction. I viewed it as a stress reliever. I tried to give every excuse for it. I did not want to think it was an actual addiction. As time progressed I realize just how much of an addiction it was to me. I started to spend all of my money on pornographic material. I would drive an hour to go purchase it so I would not see anyone who knew me. I was addicted. Truthfully, I was locked in a jail cell of emotion and perversion. My mind was being raped daily by the images I watched. I was a man most miserable who was too afraid to talk to anyone about it. I lived in such fear that I would be judged.

So, what about the church? Wouldn't they be open to listen and help me with the darkness of my heart? One would imagine they would, right? Honestly, I can only answer this question based on my own experience. I did not feel comfortable "laying all of my problems at the altar" because I knew "altar workers" were gossipers. I knew the pastor was just as carnal as the drunk man on the corner. I trusted him as far as I could throw him and that was not very far. I went to different men's groups. Men would talk about their struggles, but I felt like mine was worse. I felt like my sin was dirtier. I was addicted to pornography. It was not just pornography; it was every kind you could imagine. I was still the clean cut boy who could easily slip under the radar because I learned how to talk my way out of anything. I would try to create brotherhoods and friendships where I could share my life and everything in it, but none of them would last. I would get to the point where I closed up because I did not want anyone to know my struggles and judge me for them. I needed the judgment. I needed someone to confront me and patiently teach me the truth. But I was silent. I did not want my silent exploration of my sexual identity and fulfillment of my sexual fantasies to cause me to run from the very place I desired to go for help—the church. I knew pornography, the sin in my heart, and perverse conversations were instrumental to my continuous questioning of my identity. Was that enough to stop me from doing what I was doing? Absolutely not! I figured my silent suffering was better than my public humiliation. Unfortunately, I was going down a path where I would be humiliated and my integrity would be ruined. Darkness became my home as I tried to appear "normal" and dispel any ideas that I might be different. I am so thankful for the Light!

I love John 3:16, but it was actually John 3:20 that opened my eyes and caused me to weep. Here is what it says:

> "16 For God so loved the world, that He gave His begotten Son, that whoever believes in Him shall not perish, but have eternal life. 17 For God did not send the Son into the world to judge the world, but that the world might be saved through Him. 18 He who believe in Him is not judged; he who does not believe has been judged already, because he has

not believed in the name of the only begotten Son of God. 19 This is the judgment, that the Light has come into the world, and men loved the darkness rather than the Light, for their deeds we're evil. 20 For everyone who does evil hates the Light, and does not one to the Light for fear that his deeds will be exposed. 21 But he who practices the truth comes to the Light, so that his deeds may be manifested as having been wrought in God."(NASB)

After I was drawn by the Father I began to see the evil of my ways. He opened my eyes to the dangerous life I was living. I soon came to the realization that I was the man who recognized the coming of the Light but refused to step all the way into it because I feared being exposed. I feared that I would have to stop my perverse practices. I did not want to let them go. I wanted them. I really wanted to continue. However, I wanted to live for Christ. I was conflicted in a very real battle between the flesh and the Spirit.

Let me not try to fool you; I am still conflicted with that battle between the flesh and the Spirit. Like Paul, I know what I should do but I am conflicted with what I should not do. I know the way I should act but I'm conflicted with the way I want to act. I am conflicted. I am grossly conflicted. The very things I want to do, I don't. And the very things I do not want to do, I do. I am a man most miserable.

Honestly, I am conflicted with writing these words right now. I know the judgment will come because of many things I am sharing and will share with you. When I first knew of my calling into pastoral ministry I cried out to God to help me never be closed off from reality. I did not want to cover up the real issues of my heart and life just so I could please people or satisfy some unrealistic expectation of a title or position I never asked for. I never want to be so cut off from reality that I begin to live my life as if it was a fantasy.

You probably think the life of God's servant is perfect. Well, it is not. Well, mine is not. I wish it was, but it is not. I'm crying right now as I write these words because I have been called to lead and shepherd people but there are times when I feel inadequate and unfit to perform the task I have been given. I wish I could be as perfect as some appear to be, but that is not my reality. Social media paints an excellent portrait of false perfection, but it is only a snapshot of a person's life. It does not encompass the stresses and difficulties. It does not capture the difficult moments of depression and embarrassment. "Kill me now!" are the words I have spoken to the Lord on so many occasions.

Years ago I told an older man about my desire to learn how to be a man. Honestly, I wanted to be fathered. I remember searching for reading material to help me understand my desire to have a man lead me, guide me, affirm me, and help me find my identity. I heard countless sermons on God the Father, and I believed the truth that was preached about Him. Although I understand His ability and desire to father me spiritually, I desired a physical fatherhood—a fatherhood that could be felt, heard, seen, and imitated. Was that too much to ask for?

As I stated in an earlier chapter, my father was present, but silent. His words were few. I wanted, and needed, a substitute in my life. I went in search of mentors to lead me. It would seem like many of them had too much time for everything else except me even though they stated a desire to lead me. I did not understand why they left me stranded at that time, but I definitely understand it now. I look at my own life and the young men I do my best to mentor. It is not an easy task. I am the husband to an amazing wife, a father, a pastor to a maturing church, a business owner, and author. The work is taxing by itself, and the church demands a great deal from me. Finding the perfect balance can be difficult. Mentoring other young men can be very difficult. Many of them do not understand the difficulty. Nevertheless, I understand both sides of the paradigm. I understand the heaviness of responsibility and the strong desire to be fathered. I get it.

The Church can no longer remain silent about the issues of sexual identity and sexual attraction. This problem is growing within the Church. Many hear and know the Word of God, but they suffer silently. They silently shed their tears and their cries go unheard. We must take the blinders off our eyes and discuss the issues many face, which include same-sex attraction and bisexuality. We must teach that attraction should not drive sexuality; the truth of the Scripture must drive it! Renewing the mind, which is an important element to our Christian faith, is the process where our old ideas and thoughts are purged and changed to agree to the truth of Scripture. We would never encourage a murderer to remain a murderer. In the same way, we cannot accept the lie that says men and women who have a certain attraction must live that way. We are all born into sin; that is a truth we cannot ignore. Although we born that way, we are not supposed to remain that way. It is true that God calls us as we are—with twisted attractions, filthy thoughts, and a heart full of sin—but He does not expect for us to remain that way.

I have met men who have had an attraction for transsexuals, women who have desired to have lesbian affairs, older men who expressed their desire to have sex with animals, and so much more. All of these people were church-going folks who were too afraid to confess their darkest desires because of ridicule. It took shame for many of them to finally confess, and some chose to deny their actions even though the evidence was there. The Church can no longer harbor sin, and religion cannot hide those who choose to practice it. It must be exposed and confessed! There is true freedom in confession.

I look over the entire Church in our day and my heart is grieved. I weep daily over the condition of the Body, but I am not discouraged. God restores His people; He covers, delivers, exposes, heals, builds and sanctifies. We are His church, and we will be just fine. Nevertheless, I notice our current condition. I see women taking a place in the church they were not created to have—a place of headship. Adam was first created, then Eve. His headship was ordained first. It is not one of dominance or prideful arrogance. It is performed out of love, respect and submission unto God. The presence of women within the Church today is large. Where have our men gone? Where are they? I have asked that question for years. I provided an answer for it and write an entire chapter devoted to it in my book *So, You Want to be a Man?* I encourage you to get the book and read it for yourself. I do want to take one idea presented in that book and raise it here for you to consider. One of my key points was found in this truth:

Men are committed to what they love the most. In actuality, both men and women are; however, let's deal with the man right now.

There is an old practice of war that holds a great deal of symbolism today. In the midst of war, a soldier would sever the head from the body of his foe. Cutting off the head symbolized the removal of the headship. I want you to understand how important this practice is in our world. Ephesians 5:23 reads *"For the husband is the head of the wife, as Christ also is the head of the church, He Himself being the Savior of the body."* Cutting off the head eliminates authority. It brings chaos. It brings calamity and disorder. It disturbs the very order of God. The enemy has been after our men since the beginning of time, and his special weapon of choice has been the woman. Notice how the serpent went to Eve, not Adam. He went to seduce Eve to defy God. That was an indirect severing of the head. He defied the authority and headship of the man by going first to the woman. He used the woman to then influence the man. Adam shows how he allowed himself to be influenced by the woman in Genesis 3:12. It reads, *"The man said, "The woman whom You gave to be with me, she gave me from the tree, and I ate."*

Many argue, as do I, the carelessness of the man to allow the serpent to speak with the woman, but I cannot emphasize the importance found in this particular verse. Adam placed the blame on the woman, not the serpent. He did what most men do today. He stood back, allowed the enemy to influence the woman and allowed the woman to influence him. God responded to Adam in Genesis 3:17 saying, *"Then to Adam He said, "Because you have listened to the voice of your wife, and have eaten from the tree about which I commanded you, saying, 'You shall not eat from it';"* The important aspect of His words are that He addressed the issue of Adam listening to his wife instead of following the commands of God.

I do not want to get away from the point I am making here about the desire to be fathered and not allowing it cause me to suffer in silence. But the influence of women in the church has, in many ways, emasculated the men. Like Adam, men see the action and leadership of women, so they sit back to do nothing. They allow the women to lead the family, the church, the office, and the home. They say nothing, do nothing, and provide no assistance except in a role they were not created for men to be portraying, which is the helpmeet.

We have a large part of our church today that is filled with homosexuality and effeminacy. The other groups of men are chasing women and power. They gather for themselves teachers that will encourage their perversion and lead them on a path of worldly accumulation and happiness, not eternal hope and holiness. The lack of true godly men has created a major deficit in those who can properly mentor and disciple the younger generation of men. In fact, the older men have a special responsibility to teach and train the younger men, but that has not happened. They are not teaching partly because many of them do not know enough to properly teach.

I recently met another man who began to confide in me. He said, "Cornelius, I desired to be fathered." Those words stung my heart. I felt like I was the only one. But after his conversation I quickly learned that there is an entire silent community of men who desire to be fathered and affirmed, both spiritually and physically. His desires to be fathered were cut short after learning that the one he desired to father him only wanted to use him. I have heard a similar story from so many men over the years. I have experienced it myself. Nonetheless, my desire to be fathered has not died away.

I have argued with God countless times about my desires, both righteous and unrighteous. I did not create me; therefore, I felt it was unfair for me to have to figure out my thoughts and stay in right alignment to what is holy and pure. But I am encouraged that God provides a way of escape. I have grown tired of living like a prisoner in my thoughts. I have second-guessed my faith many times because of my struggles, and I second-guessed the Church because of its lack of transparency and openness about sin, temptation, and worldly struggles. Nonetheless, we were made to battle and to war. Our battle is not carnal; it is spiritual. And we must fight. We must fight with everything within us. We must resist temptation, not give in to it.

As for me, I have been asked if I am only pretending in my marriage and as a preacher because of those perverse desires. I, like all men, have my own struggles, but I will not be a casualty to them. I refuse to be a casualty! I simply refuse. I am not sheltering any feelings or trying to bury the actions my wicked heart conceives. I am simply living a life of purity and honor to the Lord. I believe the Gospel I preach, and I will die working to protect the purity of it. I am restrained by His love from doing anything that is dishonorable and brings shame to Him, my witness, my family and the Church. He restrains me from ungodliness and compels me to accomplish His will by His strength for His glory. That is shouting material right there. That is enough to put this book down and just praise Him. He preserves you! He restrains you! He compels you! He gives you strength! And He will supply you with everything you need to accomplish His will.

And although my desire to be fathered still lingers at times, I am encouraged that He sustains me in my times of weakness. He teaches me in my times of ignorance. He guides me when I am lost. He restores me when I am wasting away. He lifts me when I am down. He comforts me in my moments of displeasure. He has shown me that He desires me to Himself so that no man can boast in saying they are responsible for what He has done. He has used me, a man who is presumed foolish to this world because of my lack of educational degrees and schooling, to confound those who are earthly wise. He took me, a man who is considered the least of society because of my lackluster upbringing, to preach the Good News to the noble. I can only boast in the Lord.

Trust Him. Set your struggles at the altar and trust Him. Do you have an altar in your home? If not, create one. It could be a closet, a room, a carpeted area in the corner. Just make a space and dedicate it to the Lord. That is the safe place you run to when you are seeking Him. Cry out to Him. Confess what is on your heart right now. Tell Him all those things you have not told anyone else. It is time for you to let it go and stop struggling in silence. Trust Him.

Chapter 11

WORRYING

Do you worry a lot? I could not finish this book without writing directly to the worrier. I know that life of worrying because I lived it for so many years. I worried about how I was going to pay my bills. I worried about I was going to measure up as a father and husband. I worried about whether or not I would make it to my destination. I worried about what people thought about me. My insecurities and unwillingness to trust God caused me to worry. Honestly, I did not know how to trust God when I did not know Him. It is difficult to trust someone you do not know. That could very well be your problem. I have probably heard people tell you to trust God, but that is not an easy task when you do not fully know Him for yourself.

Men like David, Noah, and Abraham had faith in God. Their faith continued to grow as they obeyed Him and got to know Him more. Prayer and fasting is a great way to lessen the distractions around you and really focus on developing your relationship with God. Clear your schedule, find a quiet place, and pour your heart out to God. I love to play worship music in the background. I let out what is in my heart and confess those offenses I tried to hide from everyone else. Continuous obedience helps you to grow in trust. Continue to converse with and obey

God. The trust will develop over time.

> "For this reason I say to you, do not be worried about your life, as to what you will eat or what you will drink; nor for your body, as to what you will put on. Is not life more than food, and the body more than clothing? "Look at the birds of the air, that they do not sow, nor reap nor gather into barns, and yet your heavenly Father feeds them. Are you not worth much more than they? "And who of you by being worried can add a single hour to his life? "And why are you worried about clothing? Observe how the lilies of the field grow; they do not toil nor do they spin, yet I say to you that not even Solomon in all his glory clothed himself like one of these. "But if God so clothes the grass of the field, which is alive today and tomorrow is thrown into the furnace, will He not much more clothe you? You of little faith! "Do not worry then, saying, 'What will we eat?' or 'What will we drink?' or 'What will we wear for clothing?' "For the Gentiles eagerly seek all these things; for your heavenly Father knows that you need all these things. "But seek first His kingdom and His righteousness, and all these things will be added to you. "So do not worry about tomorrow; for tomorrow will care for itself. Each day has enough trouble of its own." (Matthew 6:25-34, NASB)

To worry is to be troubled and to feel uneasy or concerned about something that has yet to happen. Jesus warns us not to worry about our lives. Unfortunately, we read His words and continue to worry about useless things. We worry about the bills, gas prices, money, children, diseases, spouse, natural disasters, where you live, and all the many cares of life. The media helps to spread a message of fear, which causes a great deal of worry. Most times the news spreads stories of murder, rape, disaster, and calamity. Oftentimes they replay their message of fear over and over again with different commentators. They highlight it until it causes mass chaos. You must realize that watching it influences you, increasing your worry about something that you should not be concerned about. They want to tell you why you should be concerned and worried. Jesus tells you to quiet the distractions and focus on Him.

Worrying causes us to make permanent decisions based on temporary emotions. You get emotional about a temporary situation like an unexpected bill. You look at the money in your account and realize you do not have enough. You fail to realize that you will have enough provision to pay the bill and be able to eat. You fail to look to God for provision. Instead you run to pawn your title to get a little extra cash. Then you realize that you made a big mistake seeing and now the title pawn has placed you in serious debt. The interest is more than what your car title is actually worth. They have trapped you in a money pit that could have been avoided. You may ask, "Well, what should I done?" And I respond, "You must trust God."

I had a father come to me totally distraught because he did not know how he was going to feed his family. I understood his pain. He was not a lazy man. He had a job, but it did not pay enough. I asked him if his family had any food at home. He told me the food was not much. In talking to him I realized that his kitchen was filled with food; it was not food he wanted to eat. God provided for his family to eat. He just wanted the provision to match his taste preferences for dinner.

I will never forget what happened to me when I was single and living on my own. I had very little money left over after I paid my bills. I went to God complaining about what I did not have. I told Him that I needed more—a lot more! He reminded me of all of the areas in my life I was subsidizing my wants, not my necessities. I was paying for a smartphone that I did not really need. I was driving a foreign car that I could not really afford. I was paying a very high insurance rate because I did not know how to follow instructions and obey the speed limit. I was living in a townhouse with more bedrooms than I needed. I could only sleep in one of them at a time. I had a lot of waste, and I needed God to show me those things. Finally, He brought me to a very stark reality. He began to show me how He planted the sun in the right place, arranged the rain to fall at the appropriate time, provided the soil as lodging for the seeds, and so much more. If I really wanted to have food all I had to do was get seeds and grow it. That sounds cumbersome, does it not! Nevertheless, it is true. We do not worry about doing that in our day. Everything must be fast. The grits must be instant; the food, fast; the oatmeal, quick. We do not want to wait for anything. The idea of waiting for a tree to grow is crazy to many people in this world today, but that is a process we should all be thankful for. The supermarkets are not our source for our supply. God supplies, and we must never forget it.

Worrying is never meaningful; it accomplishes nothing. It will not help you solve a problem. It will not help you bring about a solution. It serves absolutely no purpose. It does bring on much heaviness because of the fear and/or sorrow and grief from the situation.

We are commanded in Scripture to think on what is pure and lovely (Philippians 4:6-7). It would do you well to turn off your television, turn off social media, and stop digesting all the fear-filled news of our day. Stop looking at the pictures that make you covet what others have.

Just think where you would be right now if you truly trusted God with everything? Think about what you could be doing if you released the worry and just believed that God would provide for you as He has done for all of His servants. I dare you to cast all of your care on God and truly let go of all the things you have been worried about. Let go of the frustrations you have and the discontentment. Realize that your frustrations are birthed from your expectations not being met. You only become frustrated when you know someone or something does not meet your expectations. You solve that problem by not placing reasonable expectations on other people and things. People are imperfect. They will fail you. You have to let it all go. The worry will continue to tear you down until it kills you. It will keep you stagnate in life. Release it to God once and for all. Just let it go and realize that you are not alone.

Chapter 12

I AM NOT STRANGE

I am reminded of times in my life where I felt discouraged and isolated because of the perverse thoughts that went through my mind. I would share my feelings with other believers. I had one guy to ask me if I was truly saved because of my ungodly thoughts. He wanted to know if I truly gave my heart to Christ and fully surrendered to Him. His questions, although asked with good intentions, came off as demeaning and degrading. It placed him at a place of superiority where he had the authority to question my salvation because of the ungodly feelings that infiltrated through my mind on a daily basis. His questions sent me into solitude where I began to question God and my entire faith. "Am I really saved?" was the question I asked myself over and over again. Did I truly confess Jesus as my Lord and Savior? I was confused. I began to feel like my entire faith was a sham. I felt afraid. And I felt alone.

I realized early on that there was a battle raging in my heart. It is a battle where I know what to do, but I choose not to do it. It is a battle where the enemy inflames ungodly desires in your heart and tries to convince you that you are alone in fighting them. It is a battle where you begin to think everyone else is perfect because of their appearance, wisdom and leadership title. I felt like my constant struggles made me less of a Christian. I felt so downcast that I did not feel like a Christian at all. That was at a time where I was basing my salvation on how I felt instead of my faith. I felt like I was strange for even thinking the ungodly things. I did not feel like I planted those lustful desires in my heart. There were mornings where I would wake up thinking about sex. I prayed before I went to sleep and studied my Bible. There were days I would listen to worship music while praying in my heavenly tongue. I would weep and cry out to the Lord. Then, I would get up, go to the store and lust after the person who was walking in front of me. I would undress the person with my eyes. I could not figure out what was wrong with me. Then, I would go to a service and sit amongst other believers. Everyone seemed like they had it all together. I felt abandoned and lost. There were times where I could not concentrate even while the sermon was being preached. I was too busy thinking about sex and other gluttonous desires. I felt trapped. I would cry out to God to give me wisdom concerning these desires. I needed assistance. I needed it more than anything. I was tired of feeling alone.

1 Peter 4:12-13 reads *"Beloved, do not be surprised at the fiery ordeal among you, which comes upon you for your testing, as though some strange thing were happening to you; but to the degree that you share the sufferings of Christ, keep on rejoicing, so that also at the revelation of His glory you may rejoice with exultation."* Those particular verses gave me peace. Jesus overcame all temptations. He walked amongst us as a perfect, sinless man. Many would argue that He was fully capable seeing that He is both God and man. However, the very nature He took on when coming to dwell

amongst us was one of endurance and prevailing power. Although He was tempted, He did not give in to those temptations. He suffered the testing in strength and focus to overcome all of it. Praise Him! He remained spotless so He could be the perfect sacrifice to bear the burden of damnation that was meant for all of us. Hallelujah! What really warms my heart is to know He succeeded. He did not give in to the temptation. In fact, He took the way of escape out of every temptation. 1 Corinthians 10:13 reads *"No temptation has overtaken you but such as is common to man; and God is faithful, who will not allow you to be tempted beyond what you are able, but with the temptation will provide the way of escape also, so that you will be able to endure it."* Praise Him! God is faithful to provide a way of escape from temptation. That is a freeing verse that I continue to say over and over again in my head. I say it throughout my day.

I remember walking down the streets of Manhattan. I was on 5th Avenue walking and praying in my heavenly language. My heart was deeply burdened at the sin all around me. My wife and I were there for a speaking engagement. She was out to lunch with a friend, and I decided to go for a walk. I sensed the spiritual heaviness as soon as I walked out of my hotel. The complete disregard for God was evident in the people. I was walking through stores praying and talking to different people who would indulge me with conversation. As I walked along the street I began to pray louder. I got nervous thinking that people thought I was crazy. As I am praying, I encounter a public display of nudity between two persons. Their actions were deliberate. My praying turned to gleeful enjoyment—almost. "Sex! Look, there's sex!" I was so intrigued by the display that I forgot the mission I was on to pray against those very acts of bold sinful acts.

In a moment's notice, I felt the Spirit of God arrest me into conviction. That one scene robbed me of the short-lived innocence I was experiencing in my walk with Christ. Most importantly, it distracted me from the mission I was supposed to be on as I walked those streets. I turned away from the act and walked in the other direction. As I walked, I was faced with a very real battle in my mind. Surprisingly, it was not a sexual battle. It was a battle between me feeling like less of a child of God because I stopped to watch their foolishness and feeling relieved because God provided a way of escape. As I walked, I felt the urge to jump, shout and thank God for delivering me out of temptation. I thanked Him in the middle of the sidewalk as people passed me by. The streets were crowded. I am sure I hit a couple people, but it was in that moment that I was so joyful. I knew the Spirit of God was with me and the evidence was His convicting power. From that moment I knew the grace and mercy of God because He provided me the strength to escape the temptation.

I experienced victory after victory. There were times where I also suffered many defeats. I would argue with myself and say I was wrestling with sin. In actuality, I was not wrestling; I was laying down to it. It was having its way with me. Nevertheless, I could not say that God did not provide a way of escape. He also gave me power to endure the temptation and come out of it without it overtaking me. He will do the same thing for you.

Do not think you are crazy for making public proclamations of His awesome delivering power. When in the middle of temptation, boldly proclaim that He has given you a way of escape. Boldly proclaim that He gives you strength to escape. Then, escape! Run! Flee! Deny! Go! Cut off! Extinguish! Do whatever you have to do to get out of the situation. If you are laying there in the bed ready to give in to temptation, run! He gives you a way of escape! Do not live in that bondage thinking you have to give in to it. Just run out the door. Tell the person to ship your clothes to you.

Do not use your liberties in Christ to continue in sin. Do not use His grace and mercy to build an argument to justify your sin. Those who use grace and mercy as excuses to continue in sin are products of a hard-heart. Their hearts are cold towards God. They are intoxicated with lust and all kinds of deception. They hunger for temporary pleasure instead of focusing on eternal glory. My heart breaks for them! It truly breaks because I know that life. I lived it for years. Rationalizing the Word of God to fit your lifestyle is one of the first evidences of a cold and hard heart towards God. I know. I have been there. But I know a Spirit who consumes with such a holy fire that He burns everything out. He torches the ice around the heart so it is capable of functioning properly. Halleluiah! That is enough to stop right now and thank God.

You do not have to live with a cold heart towards God any longer. Open up your mouth and confess Jesus as Lord and Savior. Ask the Holy Spirit to dwell within you. Ask Him to baptize you with fire from the inside out. Ask Him to clean everything in you that is not like Him. Cry out in travailing prayer. Wail out loud with tears flowing from your eyes. Ask Him to break you stone-cold heart and water it with His word so it is pliable for molding. He will do it! He will surely do it! Glory! Halleluiah! I know He will. I am a product of His power. He pulled me out of situations I know should have killed me. He preserved me when I know I should have caught all kinds of diseases. He kept me when I know my eyes went farther than they should have, when my hands touched and picked up what was not mine, when my mouth spoke words that did not line up with His, and so much more. Glory! Halleluiah! Rejoice! Boldly thank Him for His awesome work in your life. Thank Him for the work He is doing right now in your life. You might have to put this book to the side and just rejoice. Sing to Him. He is our mighty deliverer; awesome creator; wonderful counselor; omnipresent God. He is worth more than all the gold this world has to offer. Just give Him your heart right now. He will cleanse it. He can do more with it than you can. Glory!

Now, I know that was heavy. If you felt a very warm presence come over you, know it was not just the wind. That was the presence of God. He confirms His Word. His presence can be felt. Glory to Him! Glory!

I rejoice in my suffering now. I know I can overcome by His power. I know those thoughts I get that are contrary to the words of God do not have to overtake me. In fact, 2 Corinthians 10:5 reads, *"We are destroying speculations and every lofty thing raised up against the knowledge of God, and we are taking every thought captive to the obedience of Christ."* This particular verse demonstrates the power that has been afforded to us through Jesus Christ. We do not have to live in the shadows of our thoughts! We can go to war with them and bring them to subjection to the words of God. If my thoughts are contrary to the words of God then they must be discarded—immediately. I cannot allow trash to linger in my heart and not expect for it to begin to stink. I must be diligent to keep it out. The same goes for you. You must be diligent. You have to be cautious about what you are listening to, what you are reading, what you are watching. The enemy will use those thoughts and cause them to germinate in your heart until you act out those perverse things.

The devil wants to isolate you. He wants you to think you are all alone. Wants you to put on a face of phoniness and false piety to give the illusion of change. But he will spare no expense to keep you from the change you desire. He is not strong. He cannot prevail. He is defeated!

You must resist the feelings of isolation. Do not think because you carry a religious title, have many degrees in theology and preach to thousands, have spent many years in church and so much more that you will not be tempted. Do not think that your years of experience in church culture have made you immune to the attacks of the enemy. Do not isolate yourself. You are not alone. The struggles you face are not uncommon to man. Jesus overcame them, and you can overcome them through Him and the convicting power of the Holy Spirit! You are not alone. We all suffer. We are all tempted. The preacher is not without sin. The congregant is not without sin. It is a fight for all of us, but we have the power to overcome! Be strong in the power of His might! You are not alone! You are not alone! You are not alone! And, you are not strange! You are a child of God. Live like it! Proclaim it! Wear it! Bear it! Endure it! Walk in it!

Chapter 13

LEARNING TO BE CONTENT

The apostle Paul tells us in Philippians 4:10-12, "*But I rejoiced in the Lord greatly, that now at last you have revived your concern for me; indeed, you were concerned before, but you laced opportunity. Not that I speak from want, for I have learned to be content in whatever circumstances I am. I know how to get along with humble means, and I also know how to live in prosperity; in any and every circumstance I have learned the secret of being filled and going hungry, both of having abundance and suffering need.*" Those are powerful verses. I want to highlight this particular part of verse eleven: "...for I have learned to be content..." The apostle Paul, wrote this letter to the Church in Philippi. He was a remarkable man. He had accomplished much in his life. He was an educated man who was well versed in religious custom. He was a leader amongst his religious sect and a very loyal follower of Jewish religious life.

We come to know of the apostle Paul as he stands over the first Christian martyr, Stephen, after he was stoned to death for his faithfulness to the preaching of the Gospel of Jesus Christ. He was originally known as Saul the persecutor of the Christian church. His persecution of Jesus' followers was permitted and sanctioned by the High Priest (Acts 9:1, 2). On his way to Damascus to persecute more Christ followers, he encountered the Lord. This encounter was so hard-hitting and impactful that it changed his identity and his name.

He responded to his encounter with the Lord by submitting himself in obedience and denying his old way of living. He went from being an angry man who persecuted the Church to being a submitted man who was full of light and truth. Paul was not a stranger to Scripture. He was a devout Jew who knew God's Word. His major flaw was not believing that Jesus Christ was the anointed Messiah. After his encounter with Christ he was converted and he began to preach the truth wherever he went. Paul suffered greatly to carry the Gospel. He was snake bitten, stoned, jailed, and so much more. Although I am sure his suffering was unbearable at times, he learned a valuable lesson from all of it. He learned how to be content.

In Philippians 4:11-12 Paul describes his journey of learning to be content. Having to learn how to be content means it was not something that came naturally to him. I would suppose that each trial and test he encountered presented itself as another opportunity to learn how to be content. He was having to find the middle ground between poverty and prosperity; hunger and being filled. That is no easy feat by any means.

I really admire the life of the apostle Paul. Like him, I had my "road to Damascus" moment when I encountered the Lord. I was baptized in the Church of Latter Day Saints as a Mormon and regularly wrote letters to the devil about by desire to hurt and harm Christians. I was in a very dark place. Nevertheless, I had my moment with Christ where He opened my blinded eyes. Afterwards, I started a journey where I gave up all my political ambition to fully serve the Lord. That was not easy. I tried to run for mayor twice. I tried to run for a representative seat in the Georgia House of Representatives. I even tried to run for a city council seat. I aspired to climb the political ranks until I reached the White House and was elected President of the United States. This is the path I wanted to take for my life; it is not necessarily what God wanted for me. My encounter with the Lord was so impactful that it caused me to reevaluate my entire life.

I believe that Jesus does not encounter us to complete our lives; He encounters us to turn our lives upside down until they resemble His image. He does not come to be an added fixture in our many plans, dreams, and goals. He comes to take command of our entire life, not a piece of it. My journey with Christ led to me dropping out of college. That move would cause for me to lose friends, cause many to doubt my ability and sanity, and turn many away from me because they did not agree. That was difficult to bear, seeing where I came from. I was always the overachiever who was recognized for everything. I served as a high-ranking officer for multiple organizations throughout high school. I was the president of my class council from my sophomore to my senior year of high school. I even started my own mentoring program. I had more awards than I knew what to do with. I went to college with my tuition paid in full by the state. I had multiple scholarships to pay for everything else I needed. I was elected to the University of Georgia (UGA) Student Government Association Freshman Council, which was a really big deal to me back then. I was then elected as a senator of the Student Government Association at UGA. I was making some big moves and gaining the attention of many movers and shakers. I was in talks of doing some really incredible things.

I turned away from all of it to follow Christ. I did not want my own plan; I needed His. It was no longer I who lived; it was He who lived in me. Going from a place of attention, popularity, and reward to a placed of loneliness, abasement, and embarrassment was very difficult to understand and bear. There were times I prayed for death because the change was overwhelming for me. I was filled with ambition—the desire to excel and do great things. The only problem is those things did not give glory to God; they brought glory to me. I needed to give those things up. Going from one extreme to the other taught me how to be content. I knew what it felt like to be on the mountaintop looking down on everyone. I also know what it felt like to be in the depths of the valley as others looked down on me.

The most difficult part of my learning how to be content was not when I was full of food, fully clothed, had money in the bank, and what I thought a clear path for my future. I found great happiness in those times. It seemed like everything was going great. The most difficult times happened when I had nothing or very little. It is very easy to be content when you have everything you want and need. However, it takes work to find contentment when you have a need. You never really know how frail the body really is until you are hit with a sickness or disease a doctor cannot medicate. You never know how flimsy your home is made until the slightest wind comes to blow it down. You do not know how tender your car is until another car taps it and causes total damage to it. It takes very drastic moments in our life to really show us just how content we need to be with our current situations.

I have had many of our parishioners to want to talk to me

after their loved one has passed away. Their heart is open to hear something that can lessen the pain and heartache they feel. Death has its way of showing just how frail life is and how soon and sudden it can be snatched away. It does not have to be long at all. It can be snatched quickly. The assurance we, as believers, have is found in knowing that anyone who passes after their confession of Jesus as lord and savior is absent from the body but present with Him. Their death is not a terrible occasion; it is worth celebrating. The loved ones who carry on after the death of their relatives or friends have to learn how to be content with the loss. They have to find life outside of the death—no matter how difficult it may seem.

The lesson of contentment was difficult for me to grasp. I believe it is because of worldly ambition. I am learning to find the middle ground between hard work and aspiring to go higher and conquer new depths with learning how to just be grateful for all I have done already. I have a very real war within me where I always feel like my inactivity equals laziness. This causes me not to sit still or to constantly worry about something else I need to do. It places a heavier burden on my team and me. Is it an unnecessary burden? Absolutely. Being content is my solution; however, I am still on the journey to understanding it. Yes, it is true; I have not arrived. I have not crossed the finish line.

One would assume that the author should be an expert of the information he writes. Well, I am not coming to you as an expert. I am coming to you as one who is working to find that delicate balance. I want to show you that you are not alone. I am learning how to be content in poverty and prosperity. I would like to think I have had a taste of both of them. I have had to taste both of them both as a single and as a husband.

I believe being without money was easier as a single man than it was a husband. When I was single I only had to worry about myself. I was fine with sleeping in a car if I needed, but I would not be able to subject my wife to that kind of life. I have had to eat rice and apples at night because there was nothing else to eat in the kitchen. I know what it is like to have my lights turned off because I could not afford to stay up-to-date with all of my bills. I know what it is like to reach out for a loan to help pay overdue bills only to be denied because of terrible financial decisions I made when I was younger. I know what it is like to drive throughout the night to my destination because I could not afford a hotel room and sleeping in my car on the side of the road was not an option. I know what it is like to be without a car and have to walk to wherever I needed to go. I know what it is like to lose loved ones, be persecuted by family, and be falsely accused for things I did not commit. I know what it is like. I definitely know. Still, my experiences do not compare to what the apostle Paul endured. I do not want to compare my journey to his just like I would not want you to compare your journey to mine. I had to learn how to be content in those moments of lack. My wife and I would light a candle, eat our rice and eggs, and laugh together. We ate it like it was a five-course meal. We learned how to enjoy one another's company and not allow the things we have or did not have to define how we were going to interact with each other as husband and wife.

I have had to ask myself, "Why am I not happy? What do I think will make me happy? And, is God not enough for me?" I want to ask you those same questions. Why are you unhappy with your life? What do you think will make you happy? Is God not enough to satisfy your needs and desires? You have to realize the One we say we serve. He is the God who placed the sun far enough away that it can radiate heat and provide light for the day. He made sure the waves that crash against the sand do not swallow the entire beach. He placed the stars in the sky. He numbered every hair on your head. He gave you life that you may live for Him. He is not just a god of this world; He is the God of all things and all beings. In His greatest act of love, He became flesh and dwelt among us. He drunk the cup of wrath that was intended for each of us. He allowed for His blood to be spilt so no other sacrifice was needed. Have we grown so common with the Gospel message that we no longer recognize its significance? It is more than enough to make us excited and joyful. We must continuously remind ourselves of God's majesty and sacrifice.

Our anxiousness and inability to remain content and at peace is proof that we do not truly trust God. That is a travesty for the man or woman who confesses to believe in God. How can we say He is truly living and faithful while refusing to trust Him? I believe there is something worse than saying there is no God; it is saying God does exist while choosing to live as though He does not. And we live as though God does not exist each time we refuse to fully trust Him.

There was a story of a rich man who made millions of dollars in the fishing industry. He decided to take his yacht out on the water and enjoy some of the sun and cool winds. As he journeyed to his usual spot in the ocean he noticed a man relaxing in a very small boat. He turned off his yacht, rushed over to the side, and yelled at the man in the small boat, "Hey buddy, what are you doing?" "I am relaxing! What does it look like I am doing?" "Look at how small you boat is!" said the man in the yacht. He said, "You can easily have a larger boat if you work hard enough. All you have to do is take the little money you have now and buy a couple of nets. Spend your days and nights out catching fish. Use the money from catching fish to buy a bigger fishing boat. Because you have a bigger boat, you will definitely need bigger nets. Use the money from all the fish you catch and multiply your boats. Then buy multiple nets. Hire crewmen to take care of all of your boats and tend to your nets. Keep buying bigger boats and bigger nets so you can catch more fish and ultimately, make more money. This is what I did. I have more money than I can spend. I have more cars than I can drive. My house is the size of most neighborhoods. Wouldn't you want to live like that? Don't you want that?" The man in the small boat looked up at the man on the yacht and said, "What will I be able to do after I achieve all of that financial success?" "You will be able to relax," said the rich man in the yacht. "Relax! What do you think I am doing now?" The man in the boat knew he did not have everything the rich man in the yacht had, but one thing he had that made him richer than the man in the yacht was contentment. We must learn this valuable lesson. It is worth its weight in gold.

Conclusion

YOU ARE NOT ALONE

I am here to tell you that you are not alone. One of the greatest lies you will ever believe is: You are the only person who is going through your current situation. You are the only person who has made the mistakes. And you are the only person who feels shame for those mistakes. I pray my transparency in this book has helped you realize that you are not alone. I also pray it encourages you to open up your heart, confess your faults to others, and encourage others to good works. Your story could help someone finally realize she or he is not alone.

Remove the excess layers from around your heart. These words need to penetrate and dive deep into the depths of your heart.

It is okay to be weak. It is okay. The world does not need you to replicate the Superman character. We do not need you to "save the world;" Jesus has accomplished that feat already. We are told throughout Scripture that Christ is our strength when we are weak. Even a broken vessel can be molded to the image intended by the Potter. He is skilled in taking every broken piece and placing it in their proper place. You do not have to walk around trying to give off a strong image. In fact, the macho personality is one of pride and selfishness, not humility and selflessness as we see demonstrated in the life of Jesus. I would dare to say that some of you reading this book have never taken time to weep before the Lord and cry out to Him in desperation. When was the last time you wept over your sin and the sins of your friends and family? When was the last time you wept in prayer because of the sinful, perverse state of our world today? When was the last time your heart was broken because of the dishonor and disrespect others show our Holy God? I encourage you to go before God in prayer and weep. Ask Him to break your cold, dead heart and fill you with His precious Spirit. He will do it.

Be willing to be open and honest with yourself and those who hold you accountable. I have fought with the thought of suicide many times. Years ago, I sat in my closet for hours contemplating the easiest way to end my life. I felt like I had no one to talk to, no one to confide in and no one to truly understand the pain in my heart. After an intense argument with my wife at the beginning of my marriage, I contemplated suicide again on the rooftop adjacent from our condo. I stood there thinking it would be better for me to die than to continue living. I felt inadequate as a man and a husband. I like to think that I hold myself to a high standard. Reality is I am just overly critical of others and myself. That criticism and condemnation drove me to that rooftop. Brother, you are not alone.

I have fought off the feeling of inadequacy many times. There were times in my marriage when my wife and I could not afford to go to the grocery store. Our bills were high but money was short. We still have hard months where we have to rely on our faith in God to get us through. Many would look at our life and think it is perfect. Each conference or retreat we host is all by faith. My wife and I do not, and will never, charge any church or religious organization a speaking fee to minister the Word of God. If God places an amount on their heart to give then we will accept it as an honorarium. But, we will never put a price tag on preaching.

There have been times where we preached multiple days and multiple times in the day. Then, we are told the check to offset our travel costs was in the mail. We still have yet to receive those checks. However, we do not make a scene out of it. We did not go for the money; we went because God allowed us to go. Our obedience is not dependent on the check. We trust God. However, the financial strain can be heavy at times. As the leader of my family, I feel that heaviness and desire to carry that burden, but I know I cannot do it. I am learning to cast that care on God because He truly cares for my family and me. You have to do it too.

The struggle of feeling inadequate is a difficult one, but it is not impossible to overcome. Practically, I think working is a great solution to inadequacy. I believe men are called to work, and they are called to work hard whether it is by their hands or with their head. We are called to work. My most depressing moments were when I was not being productive with my life and time. Please understand, I do not mean that any idle work will be your solution. I am talking about being productive and doing what you know you have been called to do. If you do not know what you have been called to do, ask God for direction and clarity. He will lead you. I know because He leads me.

The questions that always floated through my mind were:

Am I doing the right thing with my life? How would I really know what God wants me to do? Where should I start? Am I on the right track? These questions haunted me for years as I sat in a window-less office performing a job I was not passionate about. I would stop at a large retail store on my way to work to run in the bathroom and vomit. The anxiety in the office was so high, and I would feel it the moment I woke up. I could not help but think that I would feel that way for the rest of my life. Things in my life did not begin to change until I fell on my face before God. I refused to make another step until He spoke to me about what He desired for me to do. I could not live the rest of my life chained to an office, classified by a degree, trying to please the expectations of my parents and peers, chasing after money and sex, and living with the twisted hope that I would die to escape my reality.

Your situation(s) may not be as troubled as what you just read about me. I still encourage you to open up and begin to talk about what is going on in your heart. Get with your mature, Christian brothers and share your inadequacies, faults, heartaches, hurts, disappointments, and stresses. Pour out your heart to God and allow Him to heal you. Do not grow comfortable with living in the darkness. I know your repented sins have been forgiven; however, I also know you still deal with the consequences of many of those actions. The lust that was born in your heart as a child has grown to something you know is uncontainable. You got up today and put on your smile like you put on your clothes to cover up the pain in your heart over your private actions. The guilt of your past can be heavy. The abandonment you feel can be even heavier. The double-life you are living will catch up to you eventually, and all you have worked hard to get has the potential of being lost and destroyed. Do not risk having your private actions exposed. Exposure brings humiliation and pain. We have seen politicians, preachers, lawyers, fathers, farmers, and people from all walks of life humiliated because their private sinful actions were exposed. Do not allow humiliation to become your reality. Take control of those private struggles and confess them. Bring them to the light so they can be corrected. Then, renew your mind to your involvement with them.

Verbalize your struggles. Confess what is going on in your heart. It is time to stand up and confront those things you are struggling with. You can win this fight through Christ. End the silent treatment you are giving yourself and everyone else. It's time for the new you to emerge. May God continue to be with you through this process.

Made in the USA
Las Vegas, NV
19 November 2020

11143903R00085